PRAISE FOR
THE VANISHING TRIAL

"People often ask me what it is really like to defend high-profile cases in the courtroom. There is now an easy answer. Read *The Vanishing Trial*."

Ben Brafman, *described by CNN legal analyst Jeffrey Toobin as "the best criminal defense lawyer in the country"*

"*The Vanishing Trial* offers a window into the vanishing world of the interplay between well-trained defense lawyers and the American jury. It should be read by all those who care about preserving the Founders' vision of the American jury as a democratizing force in the law. Best of all, it reads like butter."

Burt Neuborne, *Professor of Civil Liberties at NYU School of Law, former National Director of the American Civil Liberties Union, and founding Legal Director of the Brennan Center for Justice at NYU*

"Colorful incidents and anecdotes from the author's career that effectively capture the performance art of trial lawyering . . . provocative and lively."

Kirkus Reviews

"An entertaining, fast-paced, and instructive book by a top-flight defense lawyer . . . makes a compelling case for legal reform."

Daniel Capra, *Professor, Fordham Law School*

"A compelling and entertaining book with an important warning: reform the criminal justice system or it might just disappear."

John Brownlee, *former United States Attorney (W.D. Va) and noted criminal defense lawyer*

"A compelling glimpse behind the curtain of the courtroom."

***Foreword* Clarion Reviews**

"Robert Katzberg has done a masterful job exposing one of the dirty little secrets of the criminal justice system: the imminent extinction of the jury trial."

Mark Geragos, *famed criminal defense attorney and television legal analyst*

"An inside perspective of criminal defense work . . . reads like a novel."

Bruce Zagaris, *noted white collar criminal defense lawyer, author, and recognized criminal law expert*

"Told with an engaging voice and quick wit . . . a delightful, ful-filling read."

BlueInk Review

THE
VANISHING
TRIAL

www.mascotbooks.com

The Vanishing Trial

For more information, please contact:
Mascot Books
620 Herndon Parkway, Suite 320
Herndon, VA 20170
info@mascotbooks.com

Library of Congress Control Number: 2019913573

CPSIA Code: PRFRE0420A
ISBN-13: 978-1-64543-218-0

Printed in Canada

For Miles, Anna, Dax, Simon, Theo,
and all players to be named later.

THE VANISHING
TRIAL

THE ERA OF COURTROOM PERFORMERS
AND THE PERILS OF ITS PASSING

ROBERT KATZBERG

CONTENTS

CHAPTER ONE
BEHIND CLOSED DOORS

There is a new and troubling reality plaguing our federal criminal justice system. Although well-known to federal prosecutors, defense lawyers, federal judges, and legal scholars alike, this reality has largely escaped the attention of most everyone else. Today, in the federal criminal justice system, jury trials are slowly, but surely, disappearing. Over the past 30-plus years, more and more criminal prosecutions have been resolved without defendants putting the government to its proof. Those charged with crimes in federal court are overwhelmingly giving up their Sixth Amendment right to trial by jury and pleading guilty. The phenomenon has been called "the vanishing trial."

According to the 2012 Annual Report by the Director of Judicial Business of the United States Courts, in 1990 there were 56,519 criminal defendants charged in all of the nation's federal district courts. A total of 5,210 had their matters resolved by jury trial. Another 1,003 of these cases were concluded with "bench trials," that is, trials conducted by a judge, without a jury. Thus, in 1990, a little more than 9 percent of the nation's federal prosecutions resulted in a jury trial. By 2010, after 20 years of steady decline, of the 98,311 defendants criminally charged in the nation's federal courts, only 2,066 demanded a jury trial; 257 indictees had their charges resolved via bench trials. Thus, by 2010, the number of the nation's criminal defendants exercising their right to a trial by a jury of their peers plummeted to a minuscule total of slightly more than 2 percent. The number of trials has continued to decline. Data through fiscal year 2018 reflects that only 2 percent of federal defendants exercised their right to trial.

The lack of public awareness belies the significance of the problem. There are only two constitutionally guaranteed ways the average citizen can directly impact the operation of our democracy—voting in an election and serving on a jury. Voting is our check on the executive and legislative branches of government. It enables us to decide who controls these branches and to keep officeholders accountable. Less well-recognized is that jury service is our check on the judicial branch. It gives the average citizen, not judges appointed for life after having been pre-screened by politicians, the power to decide society's most important matters—life and death, guilt or innocence, whether a company or individual is to be held responsible for wrongdoing, and so much more. We hear a lot these days, and properly so, about gerrymandered election districts and other political attempts to limit voting in too many places in our country. It is a known threat to democracy. On the other hand, there is no similar public outcry about the citizenry's gradual removal as a key participant in our judicial system, because that reality has largely escaped public notice.

One of the few general media pieces to report on the vanishing trial was an August 7, 2016, *New York Times* article by the *Times'* veteran, federal court reporter, Benjamin Weiser. He reported that in the United States District Court for the Southern District of New York, which is among the busiest and most elite of the federal districts in the country, there were only 50 criminal jury trials in 2014. In 2006, only eight years earlier, there had been 169 jury trials in the district, or more than three times the 2014 number.

The *Times* article quoted the concerns of highly respected Southern District of New York Judges. Judge Jesse Furman bemoaned the fact that in his then-four years on the bench, he had presided over only one trial. Judge Jed Rakoff was quoted as saying, "It's hugely disappointing. A trial is the one place where the system really gets tested. Everything else is behind closed doors." The federal criminal justice system is now operating more and more without a key participant: the average citizen serving as juror. As Judge Louis Kaplan observed, "[I]t's a loss, because when one thinks of the American system of justice, one thinks of justice being administered by our peers."

At the same time, and apparently for a host of other reasons, the number of civil trials has been steadily declining as well. Prominent among the causes is a dramatic increase in arbitration agreements by which individuals give up the right—at the inception of their relationship—to sue a business partner, employer, or some other person or entity, and instead agree to binding arbitration should any disagreement arise. As but one example of the decrease, a noted academic journal reported a 60 percent drop in civil trials between the mid-1980s and 2002.

The reduction in both civil and criminal trials has a compounding and reinforcing effect in reducing the role of trial attorneys in our overall legal system, as skilled criminal defense lawyers often try civil cases as well. However, given this book's focus, its analysis will be limited to the impact of disappearing trials on our federal criminal justice system.

I speak from experience. For a little over four years, starting in late 1972, I prosecuted federal criminal cases as an Assistant United States Attorney for the Eastern District of New York. For the next 39 years, I defended criminal cases in federal courtrooms throughout the country. I know firsthand what once was, and in this book will try to give you, the reader, a true understanding of what is being lost. I have seen that the impact of the vanishing trial extends beyond the harm it is causing to the role of jurors. The negative consequences directly impact the federal criminal justice system's other participants, because the lack of trials also poses a grave danger to the skills of courtroom lawyers. Top trial lawyers are, at their core, performance artists. Developing and maintaining real trial skills requires being on trial over and over again, year after year.

For trial lawyers, the current dearth of federal criminal trials has two important, interrelated consequences.

First, young federal prosecutors no longer have as meaningful an opportunity to acquire and hone real trial skills. Not only are there many fewer trials, but many federal prosecutions—particularly the more complex or significant cases—are now tried by teams of Assistant United States Attorneys who divide the trial tasks. As a result, today's federal prosecutor gets an unfortunately limited trial experience, because young Assistant United States Attorneys typically get to try only *parts* of the far fewer available cases to try. Thus, when these elite attorneys leave government and enter the private sector, they do not bring the courtroom training and experience that federal prosecutors of my generation brought to their careers when they entered private practice.

It is ironic that although today's federal prosecutors are involved in a substantial majority of the nation's most important prosecutions, working at the very apex of our nation's trial court system, a substantial majority will ultimately leave the office without having obtained the most alluring benefit of the job: repeated and intensive trial experience at the highest level.

The second consequence of the paucity of federal trials is broader, but no less problematic. Young defense attorneys, of whatever background, are not getting a meaningful chance to develop critical courtroom skills. At the same time, seasoned defense lawyers are losing their professional edge, as their once-invaluable talents decay, having become less and less in demand. During the last five years of my 39-year white collar defense practice, I did not try a single case.

In the pages that follow, through the prism of my courtroom experiences over the decades, I attempt to recreate what the federal criminal justice system used to be. Memorializing my experiences in that world and depicting those who populated it is not the end, but a means to an end, to bring you, the reader, into a universe known to only a relative handful of insiders.

My approach is as follows. First, I describe how I gained access to that world, so readers can appreciate its highly competitive, pressure-packed nature. I then present the reality behind the frightening statistics by trying to recreate the era of abundant trials I was part of, to portray how that ecosystem actually worked. I'll also introduce you to some of the lawyers and judges, warts and all, who made it work. Third, I will explore the reasons why federal jury trials are disappearing. Finally, I address possible solutions that might enable us to not only preserve the best of what once was, but to perpetuate what is most fundamental to our federal criminal justice system.

In the final analysis, if the average citizen is no longer able to play the key role in that system assigned by the founding fathers, and the effectiveness of the criminal defense function enshrined in the U.S. Constitution is meaningfully diminished, where does that leave the rule of law?

CAVEAT

Law school introduces and then compels the use of Latin to identify and describe many things. Whatever its pedagogical purpose, Latin is the "go-to" spice in the common discourse of lawyers and judges, and cannot be avoided, even in nontechnical books such as this. It can also have the benefit of making non-attorneys think we are more learned than we actually are.

Caveat, of course, means "warning." Before we begin in earnest, certain warnings are required. First and foremost, there must necessarily be questions, to at least some extent, regarding any individual's recitation of events, especially those in which the reporter was a participant with much at stake. How one takes in life's experiences and reports them are always impacted by human frailty. Ego, on at least some level, is omnipresent.

This reality is humorously portrayed in Nora Ephron's Broadway play *Lucky Guy*. Tom Hanks is Mike McAlary, a tabloid journalist in New York City in the 1980s and 1990s. When he gets his first newspaper byline, McAlary becomes completely taken with himself. In a memorable scene, he waxes ecstatic to his cynical old editor about how newspapers and reporters are the only way the public gets to know "the truth." After putting up with the tirade about "the truth" for a while, the veteran editor finally has enough. He punctures McAlary's balloon by saying, "In this life there are only two truths. You are born and you die. Everything that happens between those two events is subject to interpretation." Of course, objective facts, like the speed of sound or the existence of gravity, are not subject to interpretation.

This book is a combination of the truth as I have lived it and relevant, objective facts. While certain of the stories recounted, and the personalities and events described are based solely on my personal recollections, more often than not they are the result of input from, and collaboration with, other participants in the same incident. Except for those limited circumstances required by attorney-client privilege and confidentiality considerations, I use the real names of the people and places involved. To do otherwise seems to me to be a cop-out. While this will surely please some and anger others, so be it. For those portions of this book which will likely be the most controversial, I have all underlying transcripts, filings, and documents. With respect to the vanishing trial, I present the relevant data from government offices and scholarly articles that establish beyond question this unfortunate reality.

My goal is to give a reader who never went to law school reliable, complete, and accurate information about legal realities. In so doing, I have tried to strike a balance between presenting an extensively footnoted, "in the weeds" legal analysis on the one hand, and producing a simplistic version of complex matters on the other.

To help achieve that balance, the Notes section at the end of the book provides the citation to, or official source of, important assertions of fact relied upon in the text, whether they are legal opinions, scholarly articles, newspaper reports, data sets, government statistics, or quotes. Also presented are brief biographies of many of the lawyers and judges discussed, and additional, relevant contextual information.

In sum, what follows is as unvarnished, truthful, and accurate as I can make it, to bring you, the reader, into the reality lived by top-tier trial lawyers "back in the day," and describe why that world may be gone forever.

CHAPTER TWO

THE DREAM

My path to becoming a trial lawyer began in the days following a really bad outing in Little League. That was when the reality dawned on me that I would never pitch for the Yankees. It was 1956 and I was ten. We lived in Laurelton, a middle-class neighborhood in Queens, New York, where the residents were overwhelmingly Jewish and Italian. In those days, an equally significant identity for me and my friends was which New York baseball team you rooted for—the Yankees, the Giants, or the Dodgers. Our debates over who was better—Mickey Mantle, Duke Snider, or Willie Mays in center field; Yogi Berra or Roy Campanella behind home plate; or Phil Rizzuto versus Pee Wee Reese at shortstop—constantly raged, but were never resolved. As will be evident from the pages that follow, baseball remains an important reference point for me.

My father, William Katzberg, sold insurance for the John Hancock Mutual Life Insurance Company. His dream had been to teach history at the college level, but in the immediate aftermath of the Great Depression and with a family to support, selling insurance became his career. He never made much money, as he was a man far too honest to sell people insurance coverage they did not need. As children of the Depression, however, my parents were content with what they had, which was much more than their immigrant parents. Although they were satisfied where they were financially, Mary and Bill Katzberg had much greater expectations for me, expectations that as an ambitious, competitive young boy, I readily accepted. I was always told that I would "do better than my father." This was something I truly believed, though I had no idea what that actually meant. Ultimately, it meant becoming a lawyer, providing both the career satisfaction and standard of living which fate had denied my father.

As it turned out, my natural abilities were well-suited for the courtroom. The further my education progressed, the more I realized my strengths were not in science or math, but in the humanities. I was good at words, not numbers.

The first insight into my verbal skills came at around the time I began to accept the limitations of my pitching abilities, that is, in the fourth grade. My teacher, Mrs. Greenstein, was rehearsing our class for its Arbor Day choral presentation. As we sang the song (I have long since forgotten which) over and over, something seemed to bother Mrs. Greenstein. Finally, she had each of us sing individually. After I took my turn she paused, then said, "Robert, how would you like to be the announcer?" This was the first time I realized that I had inherited from my mother's side of the family a total inability to carry a tune. On the plus side, when the Arbor Day recital came around, I reveled in standing at the microphone and doing the introduction. If I couldn't be Whitey Ford and pitch for the Yankees, maybe I could be Mel Allen, "the voice of the Yankees," and announce the games.

In the years to follow, books such as Louis Nizer's *My Life in*

Court, and television shows like *The Defenders* made the role of courtroom lawyers more and more alluring to me. But it was the black-
and-white, 1957 movie *Twelve Angry Men,* about the tension-filled,
explosive, jury deliberations in a criminal trial, that really hooked
me. Inspired by these powerful portrayals, I longed to see the real
thing. The opportunity arose my junior year of college when, instead of going to class, I spent two days in Freehold, New Jersey,
watching the legendary F. Lee Bailey defend Dr. Carl Coppolino,
on trial for murdering his lover's husband.

If F. Lee Bailey is remembered at all today, it is for his brief 1994
cameo in the O.J. Simpson trial. But by then, age and personal issues
made him a shadow of the lawyer I saw some 28 years before. His
fame began in the 1960s when he was hired by Sam Sheppard, an
Ohio doctor serving time for the murder of his pregnant wife. Not
only did Bailey get the conviction reversed, but he won an acquittal
of Dr. Sheppard in the subsequent, highly publicized retrial.

When I watched him in 1966, he was in his prime: a celebrity
lawyer whose star shone most brightly in the courtroom. I sat there
mesmerized as he dominated the proceedings. It was the first time I
had ever seen a lawyer cross-examine a witness with a prior inconsistent statement, forcing that witness to eat the very words he had
spoken so convincingly just moments before on direct examination.
Every time he began with some variation of, "Now, you told us earlier in your direct testimony that . . ." you knew it would end with
the witness having to acknowledge saying something different in the
past. Bailey's mastery of the record, precise, rhythmic questioning
and powerful presence made an enduring impression. My path was
sealed. That's who I wanted to be. That's what I wanted to do.

By the time I entered law school, the optimal road map leading
to a high-level courtroom career was both readily identifiable and

difficult to achieve given the highly competitive nature of each of the rungs on the ladder to be climbed. These rungs were: make Law Review (each school's scholarly periodical, whose members are chosen from the academic top 10 percent of the first-year class), parlay that into a clerkship for a federal judge, leverage the clerkship to become a federal prosecutor, develop real trial skills, and emerge a battle-tested pro.

Following that route, I practiced law for more than four decades. After a year clerking on the District Court in Washington, D.C., I prosecuted federal criminal cases as an Assistant United States Attorney in Brooklyn, New York, for just over four years. Upon leaving the United States Attorney's Office, I and a close friend and colleague, Kenneth Kaplan, a Deputy Chief of the Office's Criminal Division, started a boutique "white collar" criminal law firm, Kaplan & Katzberg. For the next 39 years we maintained both the practice and our friendship. I defended criminal cases in New York City and all over the country; I was rewarded both emotionally and financially far beyond anything I could have imagined. For reasons that will be fully explored later, my career as a trial lawyer as described in the pages that follow would have been far less likely had I graduated law school in recent times. Much of that has to do with the vanishing trial.

CHAPTER THREE

LAW CLERK

My first job upon graduating George Washington University Law School was as a law clerk on the United States District Court for the District of Columbia. Given the status and career building potential of federal clerkships, I had set my sights on clerking from day one of law school.

There are four levels of judges in the federal system.

Magistrate judges comprise the first level. They are randomly assigned to each new court filing, along with a district court judge. Magistrates handle initial appearances of the parties and help civil cases get ready for trial or settled before trial. Their level of participation depends to some degree on the role given them by the district judge assigned to the matter, although on the criminal side, magistrates have authority over misdemeanor offenses only.

The district court is the next level, where cases, both civil and criminal, are filed and decided, either by trial or otherwise. There are 94 district courts in the United States.

Appeals from final determinations made at the district court level go the circuit courts of appeal, the penultimate level. There are 13 courts of appeal.

At the very top is the Supreme Court, the "court of last resort," which hears a very small number of cases each year beginning in October, with cases almost always arising from circuit court decisions. There is, of course, only one Supreme Court.

Each of the judges in the federal system has young lawyers, some right out of law school, but increasingly with a few years of legal practice under their belts, serving as law clerks to assist them.

I was lucky enough to have clerked for the late Oliver Gasch, a highly respected judge, a great gentleman, and a wonderful mentor. The job for Judge Gasch brought me the prestige and resume building that makes a federal clerkship, particularly in a district court as important as D.C., so highly prized. Of course, clerking for a court of appeals judge or Supreme Court Justice brings even greater prestige, along with even greater career benefits. For example, some years ago, a big New York law firm paid a young man I know a $250,000 "signing bonus" to join the firm after a Supreme Court clerkship. These appellate positions, however, with very few exceptions, are reserved for the very elite, say the top 1 percent of newly minted or young lawyers, that is, those possessing a particular kind of scholarly intellectualism I never had. While surely not all of the young men and women clerking on the district court level suffer from as big a gap in this narrow aspect of intellectual ability, or any gap at all, I certainly felt a deficit in my interactions with the court of appeals clerks with whom I came into contact the year of my clerkship.

To illustrate, Judge Gasch had been assigned by D.C. Court of Appeals Judge David Bazelon to participate as a member of a three-judge panel Judge Bazelon headed. The panel was established to decide a constitutional issue raised by a litigant. A three-judge panel is required under Title 28 of the United States Code under special circumstances that need not be detailed here.

In any event, Judge Gasch gave me the case to work on. I arranged a lunch with the Bazelon clerk assigned to this matter so I could learn and report back what Judge Bazelon's views were and what his ultimate position might be.

At the time, David Bazelon was the Chief Judge of the Court of Appeals for the D.C. Circuit, then and now regarded by many as the most important circuit court in the country, second in national legal significance only to the United States Supreme Court. He and an associate justice, J. Skelly Wright, a legal giant in his own right, headed the most liberal and influential wing of the D.C. Court of Appeals. As both a career-builder and personal experience, a Bazelon clerkship was an extraordinary achievement, made even more so by the fact that Judge Bazelon was a "feeder" judge to the Supreme Court. That is, certain Supreme Court Justices regularly took Bazelon's graduating clerks as their clerks.

I arranged to meet the Bazelon clerk in the courthouse's private dining room, available only to the district court and court of appeals judges and staff. He had been the Editor-in-Chief of the University of Chicago Law Review. Editor-in-Chief of any top-tier law review is an extraordinary accomplishment. Editor-in-Chief of the Law Review at Chicago, considered one of the top law schools in the country, is a glittering accomplishment. From the elite of the nation's first-year law student class, he had not only placed himself in its top 10 percent, but from within that rarified group, emerged as the most accomplished and talented to be their leader. Not bad. And, oh yes, he was going to clerk the next year for Supreme Court Justice Thurgood Marshall. While to an outsider he and I may have seemed like colleagues on the same level, in the highly competitive, fast-track, status-filled world in which we lived, the gap between his pedigree and mine was enormous.

Notwithstanding that gap, I had no qualms about meeting him. The lunch was not a scholastic competition, but a social occasion in which interpersonal skills would matter as much as intellectual acuity. After some courteous chitchat, we discussed the matter before the three-judge panel.

I steered the conversation so that he would go first. He provided a lengthy and compelling discourse that sounded to me like the oral version of a well-written, brilliantly researched scholarly article. I certainly did not get it all, but understood more than enough to know where Judge Bazelon was heading and how he would likely get there. As it happened, Judge Gasch had been inclined to rule the same way. When it was my turn, I shared with him that Judge Gasch was probably moving in that direction, but still had some open issues that he had not yet fully shared with me.

To prevent exposure of the degree to which I felt over my head intellectually, and aware of how rabid (and divided) Chicago baseball fans can be, I switched the subject to baseball. I asked if he was a Chicago baseball fan, and if so, whether it was Cubs or White Sox. Luckily for me he rooted for the White Sox, and my being a Yankee fan, we spent the rest of a very pleasant lunch discussing American League baseball, a subject about which we could at least speak on the same level.

For me, clerking on the district court provided a career advantage not available to law clerks working for an appellate judge. The experience taught me how trials are actually conducted and how things work in the four corners of the courtroom, a realm far removed from statutory construction or the scholarly analyses of precedent that are the essence of appellate decisions. I was able to witness the federal litigation process in real life, in real time, and thus obtain valuable insights into its inner workings; something that was invaluable for someone intending to devote a career to trying cases in federal district court. Some of the most practical of these insights are shared in the stories that follow.

Like all federal judges, from the Supreme Court down, district court judges are appointed by the President, confirmed by the senate, and have life tenure. Their power within the four corners of their courtroom is enormous. Everyone bends over backward to be on their good side. Becoming a federal judge suddenly changes all relationships, particularly those that had been strictly professional. All but the closest and most familiar former colleagues who used to be on a first-name basis with you now call you "Judge." I am sure it takes some getting used to.

I recall a conversation I had with a former colleague from the United States Attorney's Office, Ray Dearie, shortly after he became a district court judge. We were at a function together chatting amiably about whatever, when I asked him what the biggest change had been since he became a judge. He smiled that wry smile of his and said, "My jokes have gotten a lot funnier."

Judge Oliver Gasch had been the United States Attorney for the District of Columbia under President Eisenhower, and in 1964 (in those distant days of non-partisanship) was appointed to the district court by President Johnson. Judge Gasch was popular among his peers on the court; a well-connected member of the "Wasp establishment" in Washington; his wife played the harp in the National Symphony; in the late 1960s he had been among the first, if not the first, federal district judge to hire a female law clerk; and he was an avid fly fisherman.

I still cherish an autographed picture we took together in the last month of the clerkship. He, in his 60s, tall, with straight, thinning gray hair and pale skin, posed wearing a classic, understated Brooks Brothers narrow lapel jacket, and thin tie. Me, 25 years old, short, tan, with a trimmed "Jewfro," smiled at the camera wearing a then-stylish, plaid, wide-lapel suit and broad, colorful tie. On the face of things, we were an odd couple. But of course, looks can be deceiving.

I interviewed for the clerkship late in the afternoon of a bitterly cold day in February 1971. I was ushered into the judge's impressive chambers in the E. Barrett Prettyman Federal Courthouse by his faithful secretary, Pat Wilcox. She brought me a cup of coffee that, while it helped to warm me up, I worried about spilling the entire time. Judge Gasch and I chatted amiably about an article I had written for the George Washington Law Review, a publication he read as an alumnus and in preparation for our meeting.

As the conversation progressed, he got up from his large, mahogany desk, and walked to one of the suite's large windows that overlooked the street adjoining the courthouse. I later learned that he had chronic back pain and had to regularly get up from his seat to stretch. He continued the conversation with his back to me as he looked out the window, and at the same time stuffed tobacco into one of the pipes he had taken from a nearby rack. Suddenly, he began to chuckle. I sat there watching him as he continued to puff on his pipe, look outside and laugh to himself.

Now, in today's world, the interchange that followed would be deemed by most people, myself included, to be insensitive and less than appropriate on both our parts. But this occurred almost 50 years ago, at a time near the close of the "Mad Men" era, when men regularly made remarks they would never make today. That said, recreating yesterday requires accuracy, not after-the-fact rationalization or image-adjusting edits, so consistent with the intention of this book, I present it in full, as it happened.

Judge Gasch signaled me to come over and join him at the window. I looked outside and saw this obese woman, obviously a prostitute, standing on the corner on this incredibly frigid day. She was dressed in red leather knee-high boots, a skimpy, red leather bikini bottom, and a matching red leather halter top. The fat of her body spilled out grotesquely between the garments. The judge turned to me and asked (using his typical fisherman's argot), "What do you suppose she is looking to catch?" Being the practiced wise guy I have always been, I replied without missing a beat. "I do not know what she is *looking to catch*, but all she is *going to catch* is pneumonia." He laughed out loud and I got the job.

The point of the story is that judges are human beings. What they do, or do not, is necessarily influenced by human emotion, consciously or not.

I have no doubt that Judge Gasch hired me, at least in part, because based on our interaction that afternoon, he concluded it would not be so bad to have me around chambers for a year because I could make him laugh. While hardly the funniest of one-liners, my reply was enough to establish an emotional connection between us. Sure, I was qualified to be his clerk, but so were the many other applicants who never got the job.

That judges are first and foremost human beings, is, of course, a fact that should be self-evident. What is remarkable, however, is the degree to which the legal establishment's self-serving deification of judges and a corresponding attempt to objectify the judicial decision-making process has obscured this most elementary reality.

Judges today, particularly on the appellate level, give themselves, and are given by others, impressive, scholarly labels intended to explain both their legal philosophy and their disciplined, emotion-free approach to deciding cases. These labels may describe a judge as a follower of "originalism" on one part of the spectrum, or an adherent to the "interpretive process" on another part of the spectrum. However, these designations, while meaningful, cannot eliminate the possibility that the ultimate result of a given legal decision will be influenced more by the individual judge's unique history and personal values than by his or her advertised legal philosophy. The intersection of legal analysis and personal conviction is, hopefully, illustrated by my favorite Judge Gasch story.

My clerkship began in August 1971. The District Court for the District of Columbia had been unique in the United States, as D.C. is not a state, and before 1970 had no equivalent of a parallel state court judicial system. As such, the District Court for the District of Columbia was the only federal district court to have jurisdiction over what would otherwise be state crimes, that is, crimes not enumerated in the United States Code, such as rape, driving while intoxicated, etc. In 1970, Congress passed the Court Reorganization Act, creating the District of Columbia Superior Court to function as a parallel state court. My clerkship started the first year the Superior Court was in operation, and thus, all of our new cases were standard, federal cases. However, we still had to deal with local criminal cases assigned to Judge Gasch in prior years.

I lived just five blocks from the courthouse. Since I have always been a compulsively early person, I was usually the first one in chambers. Early in my second week, as I approached chambers one morning, I saw a "slip opinion" under the door. Slip opinions were printed, stapled booklets containing opinions issued by the Court of Appeals before being published in official, bound volumes.

In this case, the Court of Appeals had issued a brief opinion in its review of a murder case that Judge Gasch had presided over the prior year, before the Superior Court was functioning. The case involved a 15-year-old student who had gone into the principal's office in DeMatha High School and shot and killed the principal. He was charged with murder and pleaded guilty before Judge Gasch. At the time, the prevailing law of the D.C. Circuit required youthful offenders to be sentenced not as adults, but under the Youth Corrections Act ("YCA"). In essence, the controlling case law mandated that the worse the youthful offender, the more he or she needed the benefits of YCA. In practical terms, that meant serving no more than six months or so at a local reformatory, an understaffed and grossly overpopulated institution. Judge Gasch had sentenced the young man as an adult and sent him to prison for several years.

The slip opinion under the door was a direction from the Court of Appeals panel that heard the appeal, sending the case back to the judge to explain why the defendant should not have his sentence vacated and be resentenced under YCA.

Judge Gasch tasked me to write an opinion upholding the adult sentence. It was my first real assignment for him, and I worked as diligently as I could, but in the end, saw no way to justify the adult sentence. I went over all of the relevant case law with my co-clerk, John Davis, an editor the previous year of the Georgetown Law Journal. Neither of us could see a way around the controlling appellate cases, or a way to deflect the logic behind them. After more than a few rewrites, I came up with the best draft opinion I could and handed it to the judge.

He asked what I thought. I replied that I believed my draft would not do it and that the Court of Appeals, out of respect for him, had remanded the matter for him to make the decision to resentence the defendant as a youthful offender instead of simply ordering him to do so. He worked on the opinion, improving it for sure, but still not, in my view, changing the bottom line.

When the opinion was ready to file, Judge Gasch again asked me what I thought. I replied that I believed we would not be sustained and that the adult sentence would be reversed. He smiled benevolently, said he thought we would be affirmed, and asked me if I wanted to make a gentleman's bet. We laughingly shook hands on our wager, one I was not even sure I wanted to win.

Some months later, upon entering chambers first thing one morning, I gathered up a number of slip opinions lodged under the door. One was the Court of Appeals opinion reviewing the YCA murder case the judge and I had bet on. It contained only three words. "Affirmed, *per curium*." Latin again. *Per curium* opinions are not signed by any particular judge on an appellate panel, but reflect the unanimous view of all. Judge Gasch had been right: the Court of Appeals upheld the adult sentence.

I couldn't wait for him to come in that morning. I handed him the opinion, he read it, and smiled. I asked him, "How did you know? Please, just tell me why you were so confident and I was so wrong." He replied, smiling once again, "That's why I am the judge and you are the clerk."

Although he never said it, here is what Judge Gasch knew—that just as his moral compass and value system made him unable to let this young man get away with the cold-blooded murder of a high school principal, the members of the Court of Appeals would likely feel the same way. He knew that notwithstanding the clear dictates of their own prior opinions, the Court of Appeals panel would want to find a way to keep this young man in jail. It finally dawned on me that just as we could not write a legal opinion adequately justifying the adult sentence under controlling legal authority, neither could the judges on the Court of Appeals. So, they did not even try. They upheld the sentence, *per curium*, without opinion, so they could get the desired result without having to confront or change existing law.

It was as though a squeegee had removed some of the grime of inexperience and naïveté from my window into the real world. The judge was right. My lack of perspective was why I was the clerk, and one more than happy to lose a bet and gain real insight.

My intention in relating this story is not to criticize or praise. If I were to guess, had I been on the appellate panel, I might have signed onto the *per curium* opinion as well. Either way, the story is told to present a reality of judicial decision-making, that is, a result-oriented, values-based approach to the law to which too few judges would ever admit. Much more on judges later.

The year of my clerkship presented a bounty of "real world" learning experiences in no small way thanks to Judge Gasch. Aware of my intended career path, he regularly shared helpful insights, often quoting his friend, the legendary trial lawyer Edward Bennett Williams. Of the many Williams chestnuts that he imparted, one I especially took to heart and incorporated into my practice for over four decades, is this: "Good lawyers master the art of giving up nothing graciously." By that, Williams meant that when your opponent wants something from you, or you are requested by a court to do something, something that doesn't adversely affect your position or does so only at the margins, the smart lawyer is gracious in acceding. It costs you nothing while allowing you to appear evenhanded and appropriate, a posture that will serve you well when it comes time for you to make a request. It sounds so simple and obvious, yet I cannot tell you how many times lawyers on the other side would automatically refuse anything I wanted simply because the request came from me, the opposition. This even included things that helped them as much as they helped me.

Judge Gasch also generously allowed me, from time to time, to steal away from chambers to watch important trials taking place before other judges, especially when a top lawyer was appearing.

On one such occasion the immortal Melvin Belli, the "King of Torts" (the objects of his negligence filings, insurance companies, called him "Melvin Bellicose"), was representing the plaintiff in a medical malpractice case against D.C.'s Children's Hospital. I had, of course, heard of the legendary Mr. Belli. What lawyer hadn't? His then-recent appearance in the movie *Gimme Shelter*, a documentary about the free, ill-fated, Rolling Stones concert at Altamont Speedway in late 1969, made him even more glamorous to me. There is a scene in the movie where Belli is in his storefront San Francisco law office, speaking on the phone, trying to convince someone from local government to remove legal obstacles to the concert. He starts the conversation with, "Mel Belli here for the Stones." Would I ever in my wildest dreams be in that position? "Bob Katzberg here for the Grateful Dead." I knew it would never happen, but the chance to meet the man who did make it happen was beyond tempting.

I watched as much of the Belli trial as I could. At a recess one afternoon, I summoned the courage to go up to the great man. He was wonderfully gracious, especially considering that I caught him in the middle of a grueling courtroom battle. Following up on his apparent agreeability, I invited Belli to lunch the next day in the judge's dining room. I was just dying to get some insight into his trial strategy, what he thought of his opponent, the judge, and all things trial-related. This was a chance to learn from a master. To my surprise, he accepted.

At lunch, to my great disappointment, Belli rebuffed virtually all questions about the trial. He was interested most of all in the nightlife in D.C. I tried to pivot by referring to the time I watched F. Lee Bailey in the Dr. Carl Coppolino murder trial. He expressed admiration for Bailey, but focused, more than a bit, on what he called Bailey's abilities as a "ladies' man."

I got much less from the lunch than I had hoped, but at least have the story to tell. Belli got much more from his D.C. experience. He won a substantial verdict in the case, and met and married a young tour guide. Today we would call that multitasking.

The clerkship was a wonderful way to transition from the classroom to the real world. It provided insights into the federal judiciary I would not have otherwise obtained. Equally important, it gave me a key credential to become a federal prosecutor. That, in turn, enabled me to develop and hone real courtroom skills—one trial after another—in federal district court, the profession's most important and prestigious trial court level.

With Judge Oliver Gash in chambers, Washington, D.C.,
July 1972.

CHAPTER FOUR
TRIAL AND ERROR

As a young federal prosecutor in the 1970s, I was in the court-room on a regular and repeated basis, trying bank robberies, tax frauds, narcotics cases, and other crimes enumerated in the United States Code. My client was the United States of America. As an Assistant United States Attorney, I prepared my cases with agents from the FBI, IRS, and other law enforcement professionals who used their training, experience, and investigatory skills to help make my cases as airtight and compelling as possible. Backed by these resources, and most often, all the time that was necessary to be as detailed and compulsive as most anyone you will meet, I would not recommend indictment of a case that had not been thoroughly, even exhaustively, investigated and prepared.

While most of those prosecutions were far simpler affairs than today's, the resulting trials nonetheless afforded me the opportunity to "do it all," from prepping witnesses, selecting a jury, making an opening statement, conducting direct and cross-examinations, right through to delivering a closing argument, and to do it over and over again. Each day on trial increased my courtroom comfort. The more cases I tried, the more my trial techniques improved. The greater the variety of crimes I prosecuted, the nimbler and more nuanced my presentations became. The more skilled the defense lawyers opposing me were, the more battle-tested I emerged.

My first trial was in early 1973. It was a near disaster.

The presiding judge was the renowned Jack B. Weinstein, a jurist revered for his legal genius, personal integrity, and strong independence. A tall, regal man, Judge Weinstein was a Columbia Law School professor as well. His treatise, "Weinstein's Federal Evidence," had long been a nationwide standard on the Federal Rules of Evidence. Legend had it that had Robert Kennedy lived to become President, Jack Weinstein would have been on the short list for a seat on the Supreme Court.

While it was certainly an honor to have my first trial before Jack B. Weinstein, from a practical point of view, he was a bad draw. Judge Weinstein, who announced his retirement at age 98, expected all lawyers appearing before him to be as prepared, savvy, and well-versed in the law and rules of evidence as he. This is, of course, a daunting, if not impossible task, especially for newly minted lawyers. Although personally gracious and always appropriate, he does not suffer fools easily and affords government lawyers no extra consideration. I was scared to death.

In the early 1970s, the United States Attorney's Office for the Eastern District of New York did not yet have a special unit devoted to teaching young prosecutors how to try cases. Instead, from a small subset of cases more appropriate to the state courts, it gave new prosecutors a simple, insignificant case that seemingly could not be lost, and let neophytes pretty much fend for themselves. This was hardly the best way to train young prosecutors, and in subsequent years the office created a special unit for new prosecutors to learn their craft. At the time of my first trial, however, "sink or swim" was the reality, and I accepted it unquestioningly.

Accordingly, I was assigned a veritable "slam dunk" case involving an undercover drug "buy and bust" with two defendants, the brothers Calvin and Reginald Smith. All I had to do was call the undercover narcotics agent, have him testify to his dealings with the defendants at their meeting in a JFK Airport hotel, introduce into evidence the drugs the defendants had given him, and then call a government chemist to testify that the drugs seized were indeed illegal narcotic substances. Really easy, right? Not for me. Although I had watched a number of federal criminal trials the previous year as a law clerk in the District Court in Washington, D.C., and had prepared my two trial witnesses as extensively as I then knew how, I nearly blew it.

My first witness was the narcotics agent, Vincent Furtado, who, in an undercover capacity met with the Smith brothers, negotiated the transaction, took the drugs, and made the arrest. Believing that the jury should hear how Agent Furtado first came to meet the brothers and their dealings before the JFK "buy and bust," I began his direct examination focusing on that history. Although today such background is part of the accepted evidentiary framework, not so then. Objections by the defense lawyers to each background question were sustained by Judge Weinstein. Not realizing the basis of the problem, I tried to rephrase the questions. Additional objections were made and sustained.

It was a really bad start. It revealed me to be every bit the neophyte that I was. I felt a level of insecurity never before experienced.

Finally, I asked to "approach the bench," a basic tactic in which the lawyers for both sides go up to the judge's elevated desk and have a private conversation outside of the jury's hearing, in an effort to iron out any problems. Unaware that Judge Weinstein, unlike most all federal trial judges, rarely allowed such bench conferences, I was devastated when my request to approach was flatly denied.

A frustrated Judge Weinstein declared a recess. Once the jury was out of the courtroom, he looked down at me sternly and said something along these lines. "Young man [I was 26], I am going to give you 20 minutes to go back to your office and figure out how to properly proceed. If this line of questioning continues on your return, I will consider granting the defendants a mistrial, and I assume you know what that means." I surely did. If the court declares a mistrial based on what the government has done (or has failed to do), then Double Jeopardy could bar any retrial and the defendants would be off the hook.

It was hard to imagine a worse outcome. Not only was I in danger of losing my first trial, one that was assigned to me because it could not be lost, but the loss would clearly be blamed (and appropriately so) on my incompetence, rather than some aberrant jury verdict. Two drug dealers would walk the streets as free men and I would be infamous among my new colleagues.

I gathered up my documents and started to walk toward the low, swinging wooden doors that separated the well of the courtroom from the public gallery, wishing that I had taken my mother's advice and gone to dental school. But, as bad as it was, I had not yet hit bottom. Just as I approached the wooden doors, one of the defendants came up from behind to open them for me. As he leaned over, he whispered in my ear, "Sheet, I'm lucky I got you!"

Having thus hit bottom, and in near panic mode, I used the time-out to speak with a more seasoned colleague who I hoped would take pity on me. He quickly pointed out my mistake and explained how it should be corrected. The testimony of Agent Furtado was completed without further difficulty and we recessed for the day. I lingered in the courtroom after all others left and went up to Ralph Sacco, Judge Weinstein's longtime, trusted courtroom deputy. A courtroom deputy runs the judge's calendar and takes care of certain of the court's administrative matters. Knowing how key that relationship can be from my days as a law clerk in Washington, I hoped to get some sympathy from Judge Weinstein via Ralph. I said, "Please tell Judge Weinstein that this is my first trial." Ralph laughed out loud and said, "Don't worry, he knows." The defendants were convicted two days later and disaster was avoided. It was an inauspicious start, but the learning process had begun, however painfully.

Compare the role of the judge in my second trial, the Hon. George Rosling, who prosecutors in the U.S. Attorney's Office referred to as "Uncle George." While smart, efficient, and always prepared, he would sometimes go out of his way to help the government. He did this to the degree that in one infamous case, United States v. Nazarro, a conviction was overturned on appeal because of his undue interference on behalf of prosecutors. Throughout my trial, Judge Rosling would call counsel to the bench for a sidebar conference to, in effect, help direct my presentation. While his insights were almost always on the money, and I was grateful for the help, I knew even then it was beyond his proper role.

My favorite Rosling trial story comes from another prosecutor, my future law partner, Ken Kaplan.

In one of his trials before Judge Rosling, the direct and cross-examination of his key witness had just been completed. The direct had gone smoothly and there was little harm done on cross. However, when Judge Rosling asked if Ken had any questions on "redirect" (the opportunity given to the lawyer who called the witness to ask questions after, and based upon, what was brought out on cross-examination), he decided to clear up a minor ambiguity that arose during the cross. This was a potentially unwise decision, as there was nothing of any significance at stake, and all Ken was doing was giving his opponent, an experienced trial lawyer, a chance to do real damage on "re-cross." He rose to announce that he had a brief redirect. Judge Rosling told the lawyers for both sides to approach the bench. As the court reporter took down every word, Judge Rosling asked Ken if he knew the two cardinal rules of witness examination. He, of course, said "No." Judge Rosling then said, "The first rule is never cross-examine a widow in a wrongful death case. The second rule is, do not redirect this witness." That abruptly ended the bench conference and the lawyers went back to their respective tables.

"Any redirect of this witness, Mr. Kaplan?"

"No, Your Honor." There was nothing defense counsel dared do or say. This was the reality of Rosling's courtroom.

My career as a federal prosecutor involved only a handful of appeals, none of them noteworthy, although my first appearance in the Second Circuit Court of Appeals, like my first trial, vividly remains with me.

Having convicted the Smith brothers in the trial before Judge Weinstein, I was tasked to handle the appeal. In those days, the Eastern District's Chief Appeals Section lawyer, L. Kevin Sheridan, decided pretty much on an individual basis who would handle any specific appeal. It largely depended on whether and to what extent a particular matter was important or complex enough to require his appellate staff to participate in whole or in part. Given the run-of-the-mill nature of the case itself, and the rudimentary legal points raised on behalf of the Smith brothers, once my draft opposition brief was approved by the appeals section, I was allowed to argue the appeal on my own.

Arguing my first appeal in the United States Court of Appeals for the Second Circuit was a big deal. Notwithstanding the basic and straightforward nature of the legal issues involved, I steeped myself in the applicable cases and prepared my oral presentation as thoroughly as I knew how. For days leading up to the argument, standing in front of a full-length mirror at home, I rehearsed what I intended to say and how I was going to say it. I even invited my parents to attend; they were up for the big moment almost as much as I was.

As it happened, on the day of oral argument, the Second Circuit Court of Appeals was also hearing an emergency stay of a hostile takeover bid by a giant conglomerate, a legal battle that had made the front pages of the newspapers. When I got to the stately 17th floor Second Circuit courtroom, it was already packed with the lawyers from the four or five major law firms involved in the litigation, along with members of the media. My parents squeezed into two seats in the very last row of the cavernous courtroom.

The oral argument on the stay took up most of the morning. When it was over, the courtroom emptied. There were just two more matters to be heard that morning, both criminal appeals. Mine was last. By the time my case was called, the courtroom's huge public gallery was empty of all but my parents, who remained seated in the very last row. It was now nearly one o'clock. As appellants, that is, the parties who filed the appeal, my opponents went first. When they concluded their argument and answered the one question asked by a member of the panel, I rose to reply. Before I could even get out the standard introductory words, "May it please the court," Judge Edward Lumbard looked down at me, waved his hand and said, "We do not have to hear from the government. The judgment is affirmed."

I had won without having to utter a word. My initial reaction was to call out, "But my mother is here!" Fortunately, I was able to suppress that instinct as I watched the members of the panel quickly leave the bench, no doubt hastening to a belated lunch.

"So, how was I?" I asked my parents when I finally reached the last row seats they had occupied for over four hours. "Wasn't my posture really good?" We walked to a favorite restaurant in nearby Chinatown and had our own late lunch.

CHAPTER FIVE

PLAYING THE GAME

By the mid-1970s, after a little more than two years of trying drug cases, airport cargo thefts, and bank robberies as a young prosecutor in the Brooklyn United States Attorney's Office, I was assigned to the office's "white collar" unit. That was the section devoted to investigating and prosecuting financial crimes. It is there where my work relationship and close personal bond with Ken Kaplan, a key member of that unit, began.

One of my cases involved a bank represented by the law firm of Shea & Gould, in the person of Milton Gould himself. At the time, Milton was among the most prominent and successful courtroom attorneys in the country. He was a civil litigator and criminal defense attorney extraordinaire. Consistent with his status, he would pull up to the courthouse in his chauffeur-driven Mercedes sedan with his initials (MSG) on the license plate. The firm's other name partner, Bill Shea, for whom the Mets' Shea Stadium was named, was one of the most prodigious power brokers and "rainmakers" of his era. They were the ultimate combination, a generator of an enormous amount of legal business and a master lawyer to handle it all on the highest (and most expensive) level.

The investigation of the bank had progressed to the point that it was time for the government and the bank's lawyers to have serious plea discussions. Potential financial crimes, including improper political campaign contributions, had been revealed. Because the potential significance of the matter required that the negotiations be conducted by someone in a much higher position of authority than I, the number two person in the office, Chief Assistant United States Attorney Edward Korman took over.

Ed Korman, Milton Gould, and I met one afternoon in Ed's office. As is typical of such meetings, it began with amiable small talk, progressed to increasingly serious and detailed case-based conversation, and ended with additional small talk. Consistent with my secondary status, other than saying hello and goodbye to Milton, I said nothing, but will always remember their final exchange. Ed asked Milton why, with his extraordinary reputation and connections in the legal and political worlds, he had not become a federal judge. Indeed, Ed said, he could easily imagine Milton being appointed to the Second Circuit Court of Appeals, among the most prestigious federal circuit courts in the country. To Ed, who later became the United States Attorney and eventually a highly respected federal district court judge himself, there could be no higher calling. Not so Milton, who responded to Ed's inquiry with a question of his own. "Ed, who would you rather be, the umpire or Willie Mays?"

Of course, very few baseball players can be Willie Mays and very few trial lawyers can be Milton Gould, but that does not stop the rest of us from wanting to play the game.

CHAPTER SIX

WEARING THE WHITE COLLAR

After a little more than four years as a prosecutor, having learned pretty much what there was for me to learn, and having experienced a good deal of what there was to experience trial-wise, it was time to take the next step and enter private practice. Resisting the financial allure of the big law firms was made easy by the facts that: my wife, Leslie, had her own career; my salary as an Assistant United States Attorney was so low it would be reasonably easy to at least duplicate; and we did not yet have children. I figured that if the two-man firm I created with Ken Kaplan did not work out, I could always go the big firm route. Thus, on February 1, 1977, we launched Kaplan & Katzberg.

Transition to the defense side was surprisingly easy. What took some getting used to was the loss of authority and power I had apparently taken for granted. People no longer automatically, and quickly, returned your calls. You were just another lawyer hustling for business, and a young one at that. On the flip side, the loss of official power only created the desire to be David against Goliath and to use the experiences and insights gleaned from being in the power position to defend clients while armed with a real understanding of the opposition's assets, limitations, methodology, and perspective.

I also came to appreciate the ironically symbiotic nature of the relationship between prosecutors and defense attorneys. That relationship can be seen in the following story.

I had a conference one day in the United States Attorney's Office for the Southern District of New York during the time Rudy Giuliani was the United States Attorney. As is widely known, before he became New York City's mayor, Rudy made his reputation as a very aggressive, extremely active prosecutor. I was there to confer with one of his line prosecutors and an FBI agent about their investigation of a client of mine. After the meeting concluded I got into the elevator, and there was Rudy. It was a little awkward at first, as he looked at me, knowing he knew me from somewhere, but could not recall my name. I shook his hand and said, "Bob Katzberg, nice to see you, Rudy." He smiled, apparently relieved, and replied, "Oh, sure, good to see you too, Bob." As the elevator descended he asked, "So, how are you doing?" I quickly replied, "Great, thanks to you." He laughed heartily, because he knew just what I meant. Defense attorneys thrive when prosecutors are active, investigating matters, subpoenaing documents and people, and ultimately issuing indictments. As much as we are their adversaries, we are also very much their dependents. As later discussed, defense attorneys are also dependent upon one another in the "white collar" world, where I lived most of my professional life.

I was often asked by non-attorney friends what the term "white collar criminal defense attorney" meant, as opposed to say, just a regular criminal defense attorney. The short answer from 10,000 feet is that "white collar" refers to crimes such as tax evasion, stock fraud, and the like, that is, non-violent crimes that involve some type of financial fraud. Such crimes are typically, although not exclusively, prosecuted in federal court. Street crimes, on the other hand, such as drug dealing, robbery, assault, homicide, and the like, are the bread and butter of local prosecutors. A more granular analysis would expose a multitude of overlap and exceptions that need not be examined here. However, even if the definitions were less elastic, lawyers with white collar practices will also occasionally represent clients in mob or, say, pornography cases—crimes that can hardly be called "white collar." But wearing the white collar brings a benefit within the profession that most practitioners greatly value, which is the status of insider.

New York City's white collar world, while substantially larger than it once was, remains confined to practitioners almost exclusively with offices in Manhattan, usually with prior experience as prosecutors in the Southern or Eastern Districts of New York, or the Manhattan District Attorney's Office. Members are known to each other, either directly or through others, and membership in the New York Council of Defense Lawyers—the only formal New York City white collar lawyer's group—is pretty much a must. Founded in 1986 by the elite of the white collar criminal bar as a counter force to what many believed to be the prosecutorial overreach of the Rudy Giuliani U.S. Attorney's Office, the NYCDL is now much larger in size, and as impactful as ever.

The "white collar network" promotes common defense interests, helps with business referrals, and allows the sharing of information often vital to representing a client. Even if I did not know the person representing a related party in an investigation who was in a position to help me, so long as that lawyer was a "player," I would always know someone who did, and I could use that connection to open the door. Members of the network are aware that today I might need their insights or help, but tomorrow in the next matter, the roles might be reversed. The result is that within the limits of the attorney-client privilege, applicable ethics, and tactical constraints, the level of cooperation within the group is high. Crucial to it all is creating and maintaining a positive reputation among your peers as not only capable, but trustworthy.

Of course, white collar clients can pay you handsomely. However, beyond enhancing your financial position, such clients confirm and bolster your professional status. They can also bring you, however briefly, into worlds you otherwise would not experience.

An example of this was my representation of five of New York City's high-end art galleries which had been swept up in a broad investigation of evasion of New York sales tax in the sale of art. As the value of high-end art rose astronomically over the years and artworks commonly began selling for many millions of dollars, too many galleries helped their wealthy clients avoid the New York City and state combined sales tax, then 8.75 percent. The tax applies only to local transactions, not transactions initiated from out of state. The tax was thus avoided by the gallery invoicing the sale to a client's out-of-state home, say in Palm Beach, Florida, but secretly installing the artwork in the client's Manhattan co-op on Fifth Avenue. The net result was, on a $10 million painting, the client saved, and New York lost, $875,000.

In any white collar representation, you need to study and learn the details of the client's business in order to fully understand what really happened, the degree of exposure, and the road ahead. This often means spending meaningful time with the principals and their key staff. Sometimes this close interaction leads to a relationship outside the narrow scope of attorney and client, including VIP access to important public events, prime seats at sporting events (including the Super Bowl), and invitations to private parties otherwise well beyond one's world. At one such private party that an art gallery client threw for a well-known artist, my wife and I found ourselves amid celebrities and other "A-listers" we had only seen in the media or read about, people we would surely never be with again. I tried my best not to stare at some of people I recognized, but every once in a while, Leslie's elbow provided a needed reminder. The one person who came over to us (other than our hostess to introduce us to the honoree) was then-Mayor Michael Bloomberg, who graciously made sure to speak to everyone present.

Whether wearing a white collar or not, there is a great deal of public cynicism about criminal defense attorneys. When Leslie and I moved to the Westchester, New York, suburbs in the late 1970s, new friends and neighbors would routinely ask me the same question, "How can you represent guilty people?" I would often reply with a well-worn cynicism, "Representing guilty people is easy. It is the innocent ones that keep you up at night." I would use this glib rejoinder when I did not feel the need to discuss what it really means to be a defense attorney. Like so many of my colleagues, I understood how crucial the defense function is to the fairness of our legal system.

For the adversarial system to operate as required, due process is an absolute necessity, and the power of the sovereign must be challenged whenever necessary. It is only when the defense lawyer can effectively mount a strong defense in the courtroom that the adversarial system is truly tested and can function as required. Simply put, without capable defense attorneys, innocent people will be convicted of crimes they did not commit. More on this point later.

Ultimately, whether it is a trial or a negotiated disposition, the process is far more important than the nature of any individual defendant. This is so whether it is the fate of a dangerous murderer or an innocent bystander that is on the line. As a result, defense attorneys often find themselves protecting the rights of the truly repugnant, representing the worst of us and taking on their defense.

For me, the trick was to create and maintain an emotional distance between myself and the client. It was all too easy to "fall in love" with many of the people whose fate, to a substantial degree, was in my hands. I have represented people who, through little or no fault of their own, faced ruination. These were people of substance, good fathers and mothers, contributing citizens who I urgently needed to help. On the other end of the spectrum, I had to avoid negative reactions to those clients charged with truly heinous conduct, and who were difficult, had no self-awareness, or were otherwise a good deal less than admirable.

On an emotional level, I made it all about me, not them. How could I produce a result consistent with how good a lawyer I believed myself to be?

The defense mentality is wonderfully satirized in a Guccione cartoon I was sent many years ago. Over the decades I saved many cartoons that satirized the legal profession and the criminal justice system. The Guccione cartoon is my favorite. Called "Attorney for the Defense," Guccione draws a bald, mustachioed man with rimless glasses six times on the page. Each has him speaking to an unseen client. In the first portrait he says, "You have a difficult case, Mr. Baker." In the second he says, "The fact that you hated your wife was inescapably obvious. Her will names you as the sole beneficiary and, as a result of her untimely and tragic death, you have become an enormously wealthy man." The third drawing has the attorney saying, "You had both motive and opportunity, and any alibi you might conceivably mount would be torn to shreds in a matter of seconds." In number four, the attorney goes on to say, "The knife with which she was stabbed 37 times has your fingerprints all over it and your suit, which was hidden in the basement of your house, is covered with blood identical to her own rare group." Cartoon portrait five completes the dilemma. "There are 14 eyewitnesses placing you at the scene of the crime and three more eyewitnesses will swear to seeing you actually committing it." In the last portrait, one in which the lawyer is suddenly smiling, he says, "Now, here's my plan."

While hilariously lampooning criminal defense attorneys, the cartoon identifies the essence of the defense role—to accurately diagnose the client's legal problems and then find a solution. Ultimately, the core of what any good attorney brings to the table is judgment, judgment based on years of experience.

For me, the first rule was one borrowed from the medical profession, "First do no harm." Most clients came to me in situations precarious enough that the last thing they needed to do was make things worse. On the criminal defense side, the ability to sidestep a looming problem before it metastasizes into a criminal prosecution is the greatest gift an attorney can give a client. In certain circumstances, with a strong enough client and good enough underlying facts, the best approach is to call a prosecutor's bluff and almost dare him or her to indict.

Early in my defense career, that approach worked for Marty Solomon, an executive of Citisource, the designer and manufacturer of handheld computers sold to the New York City Parking Violations Bureau. Marty retained me when then-powerful Bronx Democratic Party leader Stanley Friedman's financial involvement in the Citisource deal became known and a major political corruption scandal erupted. During the investigation and later prosecution of Friedman and others, Marty was strong enough and smart enough to resist threats of prosecution and other pressures to cooperate with federal prosecutors. At the same time, he was disciplined enough to keep a low profile while the storm raged all around him. Our strategy was to lay low and hang tough. Three years later, prosecutors decided not to bring charges. He emerged bitter, but vindicated.

On the other end of the spectrum, some clients—typically the most powerful or successful—had difficulty accepting any strategy that did not include at least some proactive elements, no matter how ill-advised they may have been. When these clients would dig in and resist our more cautious strategic advice, Ken Kaplan and I would invariably repeat a maxim we had learned from our elders in the criminal defense bar: "You can often protect a client against the government, but you can never protect him against himself."

Certain clients simply had an emotional need to be proactive, an instinct to always be on offense, no matter what. This can sometimes make the threat more likely to materialize, perhaps in an even more dangerous form. Again, that is where experience, judgment, and a client willing to follow your advice are all vital. Often in these circumstances, when the problem has been successfully avoided, the client cannot fully appreciate what he or she has averted in anguish and money because the client, happily, has never had to live through the looming trauma.

A case in point. I was retained by the principal of a small hedge fund who was concerned about an ongoing civil lawsuit in which the U.S. Securities and Exchange Commission was suing a much larger fund, one with which his firm was regularly doing business. My client, an aggressive young investor, was worried that the lawsuit against the larger fund would ultimately implicate him and his fund. The underlying problem was that over the years the two firms had engaged in a coordinated stock manipulation scheme, the details of which are both privileged and unnecessary to the story. My client was contemplating a series of proactive steps designed to alter his relationship with the large fund, in an attempt to head off what he feared would be a potential disaster.

I was retained with a large, flat, non-hourly fee to study the matter to determine the degree of potential exposure and how to deal with it. The client provided me with all of the relevant trading records and communications between the firms. I studied these records not only to see how substantial the evidentiary trail was, but to assess what possible overlap there might be between those transactions and the activities at issue in the SEC litigation.

When my associate provided me with the publicly available SEC litigation filings, I noticed that one of the attorneys representing the big hedge fund before the SEC was someone I had a case against some years before. She had been a prosecutor in the Southern District of New York and was now in private practice in the New York office of a major international law firm. After studying the public records, the SEC complaint, the answer, filed motions, court orders, etc., I gave her a call and reintroduced myself. Typical of the kind of "in group" cooperation among white collar defense lawyers described earlier, I explained that I had been retained by the small fund and the reasons why. With the consent of her client and mine, we entered into a "joint defense understanding" that allowed us to share our respective client's information and records on a protected, attorney-client privileged basis. She also shared with me her astute analysis of the SEC litigation and where it was heading.

Some weeks later my work was complete, and the client came to my office a second time. I told him that I could now say with confidence that it was quite unlikely the litigation would cause his firm a problem. In reply to his question as to what we do now, I said that other than monitoring the progress of the litigation from time to time, we should do nothing. He said, "I paid you all that money to do nothing?" I replied, "You paid me all that money for my judgment, and my judgment is that the best thing for you to do is not try to rock a boat that is not heading your way." He got the point and his money's worth, as the SEC litigation was settled some months later and his firm never implicated.

While resolving matters at the pre-indictment stage is clearly the best outcome, such resolution is not always possible. Often, indictments cannot be avoided, or the client comes to you only after being charged. Few such matters ultimately result in trials. As already noted and as will be analyzed later in depth, far fewer go to trial today than in the past. But a defense lawyer's ability to get the best deal for the client cannot be disconnected from his or her reputation and abilities as a trial lawyer.

When trying the case is the best of the client's options, the value of courtroom skill cannot be overstated. It is here where the experienced, talented trial lawyer provides the client with a realistic solution to his or her problem that representation by someone less comfortable and skilled in the courtroom simply cannot. And it is that realistic trial option which is increasingly vanishing from today's federal criminal justice system. This poses a threat not only to the availability of the kind of extraordinary lawyers later described in this book, but to the fundamental fairness of our legal system itself.

In my Manhattan, New York, office, 1993.

MANHATTAN LAWYER ■ DEC. 13 – DEC. 19, 1988

By Nora FitzGerald

The New York Council of Defense Lawyers has named its new board of directors and officers. The council, which was established in 1986, announced new members and reappointments at its Dec. 1 meeting. From left to right: new board members **SAMUEL DAWSON**, name partner of Gallop, Dawson & Clayman, and **JAY GOLDBERG**, solo practitioner; vice president **FREDERICK HAFETZ**, name partner of Goldman & Hafetz; secretary/treasurer **ROBERT MORVILLO**, name partner of Obermaier, Morvillo & Abramowitz; new board member **ROBERT KATZBERG**, name partner of Kaplan & Katzberg; president **RONALD FISCHETTI**, name partner of Fischetti, Pomerantz & Russo; board members **GUSTAVE NEWMAN**, of Gustave Newman, P.C.; **MARION BACHRACH**, partner of Summit Rovins & Feldesman; **ROBERT HILL SCHWARTZ**, of Robert Hill Schwartz, Counsellors at Law; **JAMES LaROSSA**, name partner of LaRossa, Mitchell & Ross; and new board member **VICTOR ROCCO**, partner of Botein, Hays & Sklar. Not pictured are board members **CHARLES STILLMAN**, name partner of Stillman, Friedman & Shaw; **JOHN WING**, partner of Weil, Gotshal & Manges; and executive director **PETER LUSHING**, professor at Benjamin Cardozo School of Law at Yeshiva University.

The newly installed Board of Directors of the New York Council of Defense Lawyers, *The Manhattan Lawyer*, December 1988.

CHAPTER SEVEN

THE COURTROOM

Prosecuting criminal cases for over four years did more than just enable me to develop and improve my trial skills; it provided an understanding of who all of the other players were and how they fit into the world in which I wanted so desperately to succeed.

Two of these insights, however unsurprising, were most important.

First, there was a wide talent gap among the defense attorneys I faced. Some were well out of their depth, yet others quite skilled. While prosecutors do not choose their courtroom opponents, I came to appreciate that there is much more to be gained in going up against a real pro. Losing is often a better teacher than winning, as we all have a tendency to assume that when we are successful, we did everything right. When things go badly, we are apt to critically analyze each element, hoping to identify what went wrong. This is, of course, despite the fact that we can be successful notwithstanding having made serious blunders, and fail even when having done everything really well. Win or lose, trying cases against talented defense lawyers simply made me better, while trying cases against the mediocre and worse merely inflated my winning percentage.

The second realization was even more important. As exemplified by the contrasts previously noted between Judge Weinstein and Judge Rosling, there was a very big difference in how a trial would proceed depending on who the judge was. Much more on this later.

But it was only when I became a defense attorney that I began to fully appreciate just how daunting, exhilarating, and stressful it is to be a really good trial lawyer. It requires intense and accelerated preparation in the months, weeks, and days before the trial starts, and mandates long nights and full weekends once it begins. Trials demand prolonged mental focus and real physical endurance, as evidenced by the all-too-common ailment known in the trade as "trial lawyer's back."

Above all, when done at the highest levels, trial work is performance art in the purest sense of the term. Second only perhaps to stand-up comedians, trial lawyers are among the most exposed, high-risk, high-reward performers. When a cross-examination works, it is there for all to see. When it fails, it is just as obvious. There is no one else to share the credit or take the blame. More important than the career ramifications to stand-up comics, when a defense attorney "bombs" in the courtroom it usually brings catastrophe to the client paying for the performance.

Your audience is the jury, 12 strangers who watch your every move, even when you are not on your feet, and judge you, and likely your case, accordingly. Few jurors come to serve with an understanding of the law, the terminology that is used (back to Latin again), or the procedures that are followed in the courtroom. So, they fall back on what they do know—human behavior—and really focus on that. This insight was driven home years ago when a colleague told me about a post-trial interview he had with members of a jury who deliberated on one of his cases. As it is such a great learning experience, lawyers rarely pass up the opportunity to interview jurors after a trial when the court grants them permission to do so and the jurors are amenable.

In the story my colleague related, after a somewhat protracted trial, a juror told him in a post-verdict interview that she and the other jurors always knew, even before he actually began to ask questions, when his cross-examinations would be long and when they would be brief. Taken aback, he asked how this could be. The juror explained that whenever he would start a long examination, he would unbutton his suit jacket. When he would just have a relatively few questions, the jacket would remain buttoned. While my friend had been totally unaware of this personal tic, the jurors were all over it.

The perspectives and sensibilities of jurors are, of course, crucial factors in trial outcomes. Counsel's ability to select potentially sympathetic jurors is manifestly important. Unfortunately, it is anything but easy to recognize individual attitudes and characteristics in federal court, where the district judges conduct the examination of potential jurors ("*voir dire*") and the attorneys are mere spectators. While the lawyers for both sides get to propose questions they want the court to ask in *voir dire*, even if the judge agrees to ask some or most of these questions, they are communicated to the panel of prospective jurors by the court. Thus, there is no direct communication between lawyer and potential juror to allow human interchange.

Each side is given a limited number of "peremptory challenges" that allow the removal of a juror for no reason. It is primarily via "peremptories" that lawyers get to impact the composition of the eventual panel. Unfortunately, this power is limited not only by the few such challenges provided, but by a substantial inability to make informed choices as to exercising same. Counsel are given scant personal information about a prospective juror, usually limited to name, age, the general area in which he or she lives, the occupation of the juror and his or her spouse, and his or her education level. So, federal court lawyers must substantially rely on their "gut" to determine which prospective jurors they want on the panel. This necessarily includes stereotypes of race, religion, education, and the like, a less-than-promising filter through which to predict actual individual attitudes.

Very wealthy clients have the luxury of spending hundreds of thousands of dollars to conduct a "mock trial" before the actual trial date. The lawyers play all of the courtroom roles—judge, prosecutor, and defense attorney(s)—as they present a distilled version of what they expect the actual trial to be. The jurors are uninvolved outsiders, hopefully reflective of the potential jury pool, paid for their time. At the conclusion of the mock trial, a verdict is rendered and the jurors are extensively interviewed to gauge reactions to all aspects of the case. While this provides meaningful insights to counsel about how to present their case, even the most sophisticated and extensive mock trial will not tell you anything about the actual people who will eventually hear the real case. Having said that, attorneys I have worked with over the years have pretty uniformly extolled the virtues of mock trials, although in the one instance in which I participated in a mock trial, I came away agnostic. We spent a lot of time, and the clients spent a lot of money, but in my view, too little was gleaned.

Most importantly, given the enormous expense involved, mock trials, whatever their value, are unavailable to most all criminal defendants. As such, the federal jury selection process is almost exclusively a "seat of the pants" operation in which defense lawyers have questionable expertise and limited impact.

How little I knew about the jurors ultimately selected in my federal cases was driven home to me in a trial before the late Southern District of New York Judge, Allen Schwartz. I represented a client, charged along with another person, with extortion arising from a business dispute. As the case progressed and I received the materials provided by the government in pre-trial discovery, the more "triable" the case seemed to be, notwithstanding that the extortionate threats at issue had been recorded and would be played in court. I was confident that I could make the "victim" of these threats anything but. Unfortunately, I was unable to convince Southern District prosecutors to drop the case, as they were confident that the tapes would be more than sufficient to obtain a conviction. Also unfortunate was the fact that counsel for the co-defendant was, at best, a mediocre attorney who would likely be an impediment in the courtroom.

I have always preferred to try cases with only one defendant, my client, in the dock. In that way I could control the defense side and not worry about either an inept co-counsel taking up time and not holding up his or her end, or sending mixed messages to the jury. Even when co-counsel was skilled, it was possible that his or her client had a different, or even worse, a conflicting defense, interfering with my ability to drive home the themes I wanted to stress.

But just as defense counsel do not pick the judge, they do not decide how many people will be indicted in a given case, how many of those charged will be willing and able to fight the charges in the courtroom, and whom they choose to represent them in that battle. In the Southern District extortion matter we had a good judge, an unhelpful co-counsel, and no good choice but to go to trial.

The jury selection process proceeded as per federal court protocol, with Judge Schwartz handling the *voir dire* and counsel playing no role. At the very end of the process a woman was selected to occupy the last of the vacant seats, juror number 11. She looked unhappy to have her name called, and from the moment she took her seat and answered the limited, standard *voir dire* questions posed by Judge Schwartz, she looked directly at him, glanced at the prosecution team, but made no eye contact with anyone at the defense table. Although I have long since forgotten the answers she provided, I recall reacting to them with a deep sense of dread. With no peremptory challenges left to remove her, and no actual prejudice or "cause" to challenge her selection, we were stuck with her.

During the course of the trial, her apparently negative demeanor never changed, as she seemed to pay little attention to my opening, cross-examinations, or summation. My hope was that the more responsive jurors would prevail. Luckily, both defendants were quickly acquitted, and I soon forgot about juror number 11. Some weeks later, I received a handwritten letter from her. It was the first and last time a juror had ever written to me. She went out of her way to compliment my trial performance and said her prayers were with me and the client. I framed the letter along with the page of the trial transcript announcing the verdict and hung it on an office wall. It served not only to record a courtroom victory, but just as significantly, was a "between the lines" reminder of the humbling limitations of the federal jury selection process.

Notwithstanding those limitations, or perhaps because of them, from jury selection through summations, trial work is arduous and filled with tension. But for me, the pressure of performing in that kind of fishbowl, as daunting as it is, is not the most difficult aspect of trial work. The demands of the moment are all-consuming and tend to blot out everything else. It is what follows the courtroom battle that has always been problematic for me. As Tom Petty taught us years ago, "The Waiting is the Hardest Part."

Once the court has instructed the jury on the applicable law in the last phase of every jury trial, and the jurors leave the courtroom to begin deliberations, the pressure can be unbearable. There is nothing left to focus on, nothing more you can do to impact the outcome, and no room for second guessing, however compulsive or neurotic you may be (and I am both). It is what it is. The hours, days, and sometimes even weeks of deliberations seem to take forever. The occasional notes from the jury seeking guidance from the court in their consideration of the case can make things even worse. Too often, these communications generate either unnecessary fear or unjustified optimism in lawyers and clients alike, rather than provide a reliable window into what the jury is actually thinking.

The Special Counsel's prosecution of Trump's campaign chairman, Paul Manafort, in the District Court in Northern Virginia provides a classic example. On the first day of deliberations the jury sent out four notes, including one asking for further instruction on the definition of "proof beyond a reasonable doubt," the legal standard by which they were to judge the defendant's guilt. Such a request is neither surprising nor unusual, as it is only logical the jury would want to know as much as possible about the standard they have to apply in reaching a verdict. Apparently, based upon these communications, Manafort's lead attorney announced to the press that it had been a great day for his client. Two days of additional positive analysis of the jury's deliberations by Manafort's counsel followed. On day four, Paul Manafort was convicted of crimes exposing him to life in prison.

While enduring the wait, everything else—even your most pressing personal issues—is on the back burner to be dealt with only after the verdict. In the interim, you, your client, and his or her friends and family hang around the vicinity of the courtroom, just waiting. You try to read materials from other cases you are working on, but cannot really focus. The client and his or her retinue make small talk if they speak at all, as they hug and pace the halls. Everyone knows that, if it goes the wrong way, the consequences will be at best painful, and at worst, life-changing in the most negative manner.

While in federal cases, the prosecution is always the strong if not overwhelming favorite, your client and his family have placed all of their faith (and a good deal of their money) in the belief that you have the talent, experience, and drive to beat the odds. You, yourself, like to think you can achieve better results than most of your colleagues, and you have to do just that every once in a while to maintain that ego. The verdict you wait for is, in part, a referendum on more than the client. Fair or not, it reflects on the lawyer as well.

Most all of the jury deliberations I experienced are by now pretty much a well-repressed blur. One, however, remains etched in my mind—waiting for the verdict in the Mark Belnick trial.

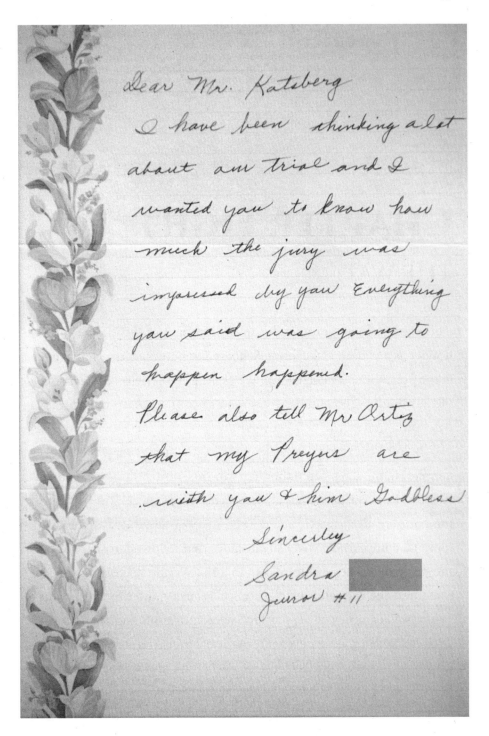

Dear Mr. Katzberg

I have been thinking a lot about our trial and I wanted you to know how much the jury was impressed by you. Everything you said was going to happen happened.

Please also tell Mr Ortiz that my Preyrs are with you & him Godbless

Sincerley
Sandra ▮▮▮▮
Juror # 11

Juror number eleven's post-trial note.

CHAPTER EIGHT

THE WAIT

Mark Belnick graduated from Columbia Law School with top honors as a Harlan Fiske Stone Scholar and became a major partner at the prestigious law firm Paul, Weiss, Rifkin, Wharton & Garrison. He left Paul, Weiss and briefly served as counsel to his undergraduate alma mater, Cornell University.

Belnick thereafter became chief legal counsel for Tyco International in the days when the then-famous, now-infamous, Dennis Kozlowski was riding high as one of the most successful CEOs in the country. Kozlowski joined Tyco in 1975 when it was a small, regional company, and over the decades that followed, rose through the ranks until he became CEO in 1992. While its core business remained the sale and installation of security and fire protection systems, via a series of very aggressive acquisitions and expansions, Tyco became a multifaceted international juggernaut, with Dennis Kozlowski its well-publicized face. When he and senior executive Mark Swartz were indicted by the New York County District Attorney for various New York State business crimes, most of which related to allegations of self-enrichment to the tune of some $400 million, it was a major scandal.

A third defendant was Mark Belnick, who was indicted under the theory that the millions of dollars in loans and remuneration he had received under his employment agreement were somehow a part of the $400 million scheme. Belnick reached out to Reid Weingarten of the Washington D.C. law firm Steptoe & Johnson to represent him. I had worked closely with Reid on a number of New York federal cases by that time and was a big fan. In choosing Reid, Belnick showed me that he was as smart as advertised. As Steptoe did not then have a New York office, Reid asked me to be local counsel and help in the trial, an offer I gladly accepted.

The evidence against Kozlowski and Swartz was, of course, stronger and far more sensational than against Belnick. The New York City tabloids, for example, had a field day with a $6,000 shower curtain Kozlowski bought for one of his homes. Accordingly, the first goal was to get Mark Belnick's case severed from the other two, that is, to have him tried separately. This would bring three major benefits. First, it would narrow the evidence at Belnick's "stand alone" trial to what he actually did, or in his case, did not do. Second, it would allow more trial separation from the other two, hopefully preventing, or at least limiting, the jury's view of them, their conduct at Tyco, and their lavish lifestyles from "spilling over" against Belnick. Finally, given the strength of the case against the other two, their top positions at Tyco, and the notoriety Kozlowski in particular had garnered, the trial of Kozlowski and Swartz would likely be first, giving Belnick's defense team a preview of much of the District Attorney's overall case and the ability to size up most of their potential witnesses against Belnick.

While I was skeptical that the severance motion would prevail, Reid was confident. His arguments carried the day and Belnick's prospects rose accordingly. As expected, Kozlowski and Swartz were tried first. The heavily publicized trial resulted in a hung jury, as one member of the jury panel refused to join the others in guilty verdicts. They were both later convicted when the case was retried, and each received a long prison term.

The Belnick trial followed the mistrial of Kozlowski and Swartz. From the defense perspective, it could hardly have gone better. Reid was lead counsel, with his partner Mark Hulkower right behind. They were both superb. They punched holes in the state's case day after day. I contributed three cross-examinations, only one of which was material to the outcome. By the time the jury began its deliberations, team Belnick was hopeful, but far too seasoned to be outwardly confident. We waited in the courthouse for the verdict along with Mark's children, and extended family and friends, including a cadre of former Paul, Weiss colleagues who admirably stuck with Mark throughout and regularly attended the trial. Mark and his stalwart wife, Randy, decamped to the privacy of the office we had rented two blocks from the courthouse.

Confirming our view regarding how the trial had gone, John Moscow, the chief prosecutor, approached Reid early in the jury deliberations with a plea deal that reflected just how concerned the prosecution was. Belnick was offered a misdemeanor plea with no jail, saving him from what could have been years incarcerated in a dangerous state correctional institution, and potentially allowing him to keep his law license and go on with his life. In addition, Tyco International would agree to dismiss a multimillion-dollar civil lawsuit against him arising from the same underlying transactions, and pay a portion of his remaining contract. It was an offer crafted to be irresistible, but in Reid's discussions with Belnick, Belnick was unmoved. I was taken aback, but felt Belnick was seeing just how far he could push things.

He directed Reid to go back and further negotiate aspects of the deal with John Moscow to better protect his law license, and to get a concession from David Boies, Tyco's lawyer in the civil suit, to receive all of the money he was potentially owed under his employment agreement. It was a gutsy move, but one that, in retrospect, seems less startling than it did at the time.

The rest of us paced the hallway as we waited for Reid to return from these discussions. I tried not to show my anxiety to the others, especially to members of Mark's family who huddled together. Members of the press had gathered in the hallway, and I tried to avoid them as well, as there was nothing to be said, and even if there was, Reid would have to be the one to say it. As a result, I pretty much stayed with the legal team or walked far down the hall seeking a degree of solitude while still being within range of the courtroom.

Fortunately, I had meandered back to the courtroom door when we were suddenly ordered to return to the courtroom. There was a note from the jury that they had reached a verdict. The plea negotiations were now on hold. Belnick and his wife returned to the courtroom, and the lawyers all met with the judge, Michael Obus, in his chambers. Judge Obus agreed to wait before taking the verdict to give the parties additional time to work out a deal.

Reid went back to the District Attorney's offices and resumed the discussions while the rest of us again waited anxiously outside the courtroom. In these incredibly tense moments, the least anxious person seemed to be Mark Belnick, who went over aspects of his Tyco employment contract with me and Mark Hulkower in the calmest and most analytic way. When Reid eventually returned to report that there was little movement from the District Attorney, and none at all from David Boies and Tyco, Belnick's calm disappeared.

Replying to John Moscow's suggestion to Reid that we adjourn for the day to think things over, in a loud, angry voice Belnick said, "Fuck John Moscow, and fuck David Boies. I am taking the fucking verdict and I am taking it now." Belnick was rejecting a guarantee of no jail, and by any reasonable definition, a very large sum of money. He was insisting on complete vindication, and all of the money he was entitled to. It was among the most dramatic and courageous things I have ever seen.

Reid informed the judge there would be no plea and that we would be taking the verdict. The pressure was enormous. Belnick refused to take the safest of ways out and faced possible ruination. What if we were all overly optimistic? What if the sensational nature of the case, and all of the terrible press about Kozlowski and Tyco, were too much to overcome?

These dark thoughts dominated my emotions as we returned to the courtroom. While we were waiting for the judge to take the bench and for the jury to return with its verdict, I walked over to one of the uniformed courtroom officers with whom I had become friendly during the course of the trial. He had escorted the jury in and out of the courtroom during the trial, and I often saw him standing guard outside the jury room during court recesses. My guess was he already knew the verdict. Unable to suppress my anxiety, I hoped he would confide his inside information to me. Good or bad, I was at the end of my emotional rope and just needed to know the outcome.

In a quiet voice, I asked if he knew the verdict and, if so, what it was. We went back and forth a bit. He conceded nothing, saying that even if he did know, he really could not reveal the verdict before it was announced. I kept trying to coax something, anything, out of him. The pressure I was feeling could not have been more intense.

Finally, as Judge Obus took the bench and the members of jury filed into their seats, the officer ended the conversation by saying, "I can only say go back to counsel table and enjoy the verdict." Belnick seemed to be watching my conversation with the officer, and I thought he may have figured what was going on. As I walked back to the defense table, I tried to send him a discreet sign that we had won, but by that time, Mark was no longer looking at me. There was no way for me to take the pressure off his back. All I could do was watch as he let out a sigh, lowered his head, and kept it that way as the "not guilty" verdicts on all counts of the indictment poured over us like manna from heaven.

Cross-examining a witness in <u>People v. Belnick</u>, June 2004.

See note on page 211.

CHAPTER NINE

TALENT

Years ago, I had lunch with a colleague in the cafeteria of the federal courthouse in Manhattan. In a conversation that has obviously stayed with me, he told me about his eldest son who had been the number one men's singles tennis player at Stanford University. As a long-ago, really mediocre tennis player, I understood just how monumental an accomplishment that was. But my friend was not telling me the story to brag (okay, maybe a little). He focused instead on his son's post-graduation, unsuccessful, two-year struggle to turn pro. As his son reported, there is a real talent gap between the best college tennis players and the bottom-level professionals on the tour. There is an additional gap between the bottom-level pros and the top-tier players who make a lot of money playing tennis. The very top, most elite tennis players, say a Roger Federer or a Serena Williams, operate in a space even further removed.

For me, there is a close analogy between my friend's son's description of the professional tennis tour and the courtroom "back in the day." The talent gap was great between the trial lawyers just getting by and those who did well. The gap between those who did well and the Roger Federers of the courtroom, while not quite as large, was nonetheless significant. This chapter is devoted to the courtroom superstars, as appreciated by someone who played the same game at a level below.

In a fundamental way, courtroom talent, or the lack thereof, is readily observable. Does the lawyer seem comfortable or tense, facile with witnesses or stumbling, collegial with the opposition or adversarial, quick-witted or slow, adroit in handling exhibits or clumsy, prepared and to the point, or rambling and disjointed? But undergirding everything a lawyer does in the courtroom are two key relationships: the one with the judge and the one with the jury.

As will be fully discussed in Chapter Eleven, federal judges come in all stripes. Some are brilliant, others hardly so; some are patient, others anything but; some are interpersonally facile, others socially inept; some are seasoned jurists, others new to the task.

Jurors, however, have no idea.

Unless something clearly to the contrary occurs right before their eyes, they tend to see whoever is wearing the robes as wise, experienced, and impartial. This is hardly surprising, as everyone in the courtroom must rise upon the judge's every entrance and exit; he or she presides over the trial on a raised platform, looking down on the proceedings, under a large, round, bronze wall plaque emblazoned with the symbols of government power, and with the stars and stripes over a shoulder.

Thus, with all of the accoutrements of judicial dominion readily visible, how the lawyer deals with the judicial authority figure, and even more importantly, how that authority figure treats the lawyer, directly impacts how the jury views the lawyer. When a judge treats a lawyer with any level of impatience or disrespect, it will negatively impact how the jury sees that lawyer, particularly if it seems the lawyers on both sides are not being treated the same way.

Defense lawyers have traditionally believed that negative judicial interference is most always directed at them, not prosecutors. A favorite old saw goes like this: "There are only two kinds of federal judges—those who smile before they screw you and those who don't smile." While this is surely a gross overstatement, it reflects a dominant defense mindset from "back in the day," one that still lingers. Of course, there are always exceptions—judges who lean on, or even openly chastise, prosecutors while jurors take it all in. A glaring example is District Judge J.T. Ellis. When he presided over the previously referenced Paul Manafort trial, he overtly and repeatedly challenged lead prosecutor Greg Andres at almost every juncture.

But exceptions are, by definition, exceptional. I cannot recall a single trial of mine in which the prosecutor was treated in a significantly more negative way than I or co-counsel in the presence of the jury. And so, you learn to cope.

Over the years I would almost always respond to judicial interference, justified or not, with, "Thank you, Your Honor." It was my way of showing surface respect, without arguing or conceding.

In one trial in the mid-1980s, this tactic produced a way to not only absorb judicial intrusion, but to capitalize on it as well. It was in a trial presided over by the Eastern District of New York's Thomas C. Platt, a negative, impatient, pro-prosecution judge who was, ironically, almost as unpopular with most prosecutors as he was with nearly all defense attorneys. Appointed to the bench by President Nixon, Platt came from a long line of Republican political leaders, including his great grandfather, "Boss Platt," for whom he was named.

Judge Platt is primarily remembered for fining the striking flight controller's union $100,000 for each hour of their walkout. He also barred the media from the civil trial of Singer Connie Francis, a ruling that was quickly overturned by the Second Circuit Court of Appeals. Beyond his negative demeanor and outlook, making matters even worse for attorneys appearing in Judge Platt's courtroom was the unfortunate fact that, in "Seinfeld speak," he was a "low talker." His soft, yet raspy voice, rarely projected into the well of the courtroom. Requests to have the judge repeat what he said would often be met with obvious annoyance, further exacerbating an already tense atmosphere. As a result, I often found myself just guessing what Judge Platt was trying to communicate—not a good place to be.

At the trial in question, among the most significant pieces of evidence against my client was a letter he had written to a business associate which the government alleged revealed his criminal intent to commit an insurance fraud. As my cross-examinations started to impact the prosecution's case, Judge Platt would interrupt, trying to block what I was doing, or at least disrupt the rhythm I was beginning to develop. After each interruption I replied, "Thank you, Your Honor," and tried to move ahead.

At the end of the case, in his summation, the prosecutor had a single sentence from my client's letter blown up as an exhibit, and stressing its narrow, literal meaning to the jury, argued its importance to the overall case. In my summation, I tried to deflect this argument by referring back to the times Judge Platt had interrupted my cross-examinations. The piece went something like this: "Mr. ____ (the prosecutor) wants you to take the literal meaning of the words in this sentence, as if that is the only way words can be understood. But the literal meaning of words can often be misleading. Do you recall the numerous times Judge Platt injected a question or criticism during one of my questions to witnesses? Remember what I replied each time? Thank you! Those were my actual words, thank you. But, was I really thanking the judge? Do you think I was grateful? Of course not. But, under the circumstances, given my respect for all federal judges, I had to use words that conveyed a different meaning than a literal interpretation provides."

My associate later told me that Platt could barely hide his anger when I uttered those words. He got the last laugh, however, as my client was ultimately convicted.

The other courtroom relationship, between the lawyer and the jury, is not only even more important, but is the key to success.

Talented trial lawyers are more than their client's representative in a legal matter. They are his or her courtroom alter ego, providing a protective layer of decency and authority against the onslaught of negative evidence presented by the government. Of course, you cannot try to be someone you aren't. As John Prine instructs, "You are what you are, and you ain't what you ain't," and jurors are especially good at spotting phonies. As such, within the confines of the courtroom, you have to be the best version of yourself at all times, because so much depends on how the jurors see you and how they react to you in very human terms.

At the end of the case, in your summation, you are asking 12 strangers to exercise their enormous power to vote their verdict in favor of your client. Everything that has occurred from jury selection onward has been in anticipation of this moment. It is your chance to speak directly to these folks, in your own words, with clarity and conviction, using all of your powers of persuasion. If you have successfully instilled in them a degree of confidence in you, your honesty, abilities, and belief in your cause, if you have even gone so far as to make them like you, convincing them to go your way will be a lot easier. If, on the other hand, you have made a less favorable impression, your chances become diminished accordingly.

Making the right impression begins on day one, with jury selection. From that point on, as in the story of the attorney unbut-
toning his suit jacket prior to a lengthy cross-examination, every
detail—how you act, how you look, what you say, and how you say
it—is being observed, noted, and stored by jurors. Their ultimate
judgement on the merits of your case cannot be separated from
how they view you.

While I earlier noted that trial talent, on a basic level, is there
for all to see, observer status takes you just so far. You cannot fully
appreciate a trial lawyer's skills unless you are actually in the well of
the courtroom working alongside that lawyer, either as co-counsel
for the same client or in a multi-defendant case representing another
defendant. It is only then that you are able to fully understand how
good or bad the underlying facts are, what there is to work with,
what must be avoided, what burdens and obstacles must be overcome, and how that attorney deals with the existing landscape. For
that reason, I limit this book's identification of the very best trial
lawyers of the passing era from the small subset of the approximately 50 or so lawyers I have actually tried cases with.

In looking back over the years, it is striking how very few wom-
en are in this group. From the late 1980s on I worked with many
talented women defending white collar cases, but I never tried a case
with any of them. Perhaps this is because women largely entered
this male-dominated world when the era of the vanishing trial was
beginning, and thus there were fewer trial opportunities for them.
Whatever the basis, the reality is that I am left with a virtually all-
male lineup from which to choose. This speaks only to the limits
of any individual's overall experience, and in no way detracts from
the brilliance of the three courtroom stars depicted in the pages

that follow.

Unfortunately, these long-after-the-fact attempts to describe their artistic brilliance on paper, especially without trial transcripts, cannot replicate the actual, real-life experience. As noted before, trial lawyers are performance artists. I can no more provide the reader a full appreciation of their courtroom work in these pages than I could do justice to just how hysterical Chris Rock's standup routine, "Bigger and Blacker," was in 1999. I am left to illustrate the power of their gifts by recreating specific instances that provide a window into how they achieved the admiration of their peers. Reputation, I have discovered, can be misleading. Too often, I have seen lawyers with big reputations turn in truly dismal trial performances. On the other hand, every so often, someone previously unknown to you can just blow you away.

And that brings me to my first superstar.

Benjamin Brafman

Sometime in 1987, I got a call from one of the deans of the New York criminal defense bar, Gustave Newman. Gus told me he wanted to refer a client to me in a big, federal mob case in the Eastern District of New York and asked if I would be interested. At that point in my career I had never defended an organized crime case, but like the baseball player who wants to play in the World Series, I always wanted to be in big cases. In addition, I was certainly not going to say no to Gus Newman, a major player and a potential source of future business. Moreover, Gus, who passed away on May 1, 2017 (Law Day), was an extraordinary gentleman. In the highly competitive New York City white collar legal community, egos are really large yet easily bruised. Thus, no member of this community can completely escape criticism from at least some quarters. No one, that is, except Gus Newman, whose talent and class were simply undeniable.

The client, Eddie Lino, an alleged "made member" of the Gambino organized crime family, was an old client of Gus's. Eddie wanted Gus to represent him, but Gus did not want to get caught up in what was projected to be a two-month trial and, frankly, for reasons never detailed, wanted to get away from Eddie. That's where I came in. The fee would be substantial, and there was no problem with the source of the money (a potential hazard in any mob case), as Lino's wife owned and ran a successful, clean, private bus company and would pay the fee. I agreed to meet Lino and thanked Gus. Gus responded with something along the lines of, "Don't thank me, Bobby. I am thanking you. When you deal with him, you'll know why." Too excited to get a big case from one of New York City's best, the warning hardly registered.

I met with Eddie Lino, who seemed right out of central casting. He had slicked-back black hair and dark, narrow-set eyes; he rarely smiled. Eddie always wore a suit, usually over a black dress shirt and light-colored tie. In short, he looked and acted every bit the stone-cold killer allegedly involved in the infamous Spark's Steakhouse murder of Mafia Boss Paul Castellano.

After I signed him up as a client, we began to spend time together, although meeting me to prepare his case was not a high priority for Eddie. He always seemed to have somewhere else to be. He only grudgingly addressed, in cryptic fashion, the questions I raised about the underlying facts. Our meetings covered minimal ground and were somewhat tense. While I was unsure whether he always acted this way or it was because I had come in to replace a long-trusted adviser, I clearly had not yet earned his confidence.

Over time, I thought I had a pretty good grasp of why Gus wanted to get away from Eddie. Unfortunately, I did not know the half of it.

It is often difficult to discern whether something is a good break or bad without the passage of time. The Lino matter, which I had originally thought to be a great break (big trial, good fee, and a furthering of my relationship with a top attorney and great gentleman, Gus Newman), turned out to be by far the worst trial experience of my life. Yet, in turn, the worst trial experience of my life—one that lasted four months of days I did not want to get out of bed—brought me a close, personal, and professional relationship with Ben Brafman that has endured to this day.

There were ten defendants on trial in the case, United States v. Angelo Ruggiero, et al. They were all charged with being part of a racketeering enterprise (RICO) as members of the Gambino Crime Family. The top two defendants were "boss" Angelo Ruggiero and "underboss" Gene Gotti, John Gotti's younger brother. They were represented, respectively, by Jeffrey Hoffman and Ron Fischetti, both talented and experienced trial lawyers. Ron Fischetti, who had emerged under the tutelage of the great Jimmy LaRossa (featured next) was particularly impressive. I casually knew some of the other lawyers, but a couple of them I did not know at all.

As is typical in multi-defendant cases, the lawyers regularly got together outside of the courtroom to coordinate their trial preparation work. Although we had met briefly at the initial court appearance on the case, it was at the opening "joint defense" lawyer's meeting that I first spent any time with Ben Brafman.

Ben was in the early years of private practice after prosecuting cases in the New York County District Attorney's Office. I later learned that he had been a standout trial lawyer on DA Robert Morgenthau's staff. Ben went on to become among the most famous criminal defense attorneys in the country. He has represented sports stars such as former New York Giant's receiver Plaxico Burress, rap artists like Jay-Z and P Diddy, international political figures such as Dominick Strauss Kahn, notorious businessmen such as biotech executive Martin Shkreli, and most recently, movie mogul Harvey Weinstein. It is no surprise that Jeffrey Toobin, a former federal prosecutor and current writer for *The New Yorker* and a CNN legal analyst, who in my view is among the sharpest legal minds on television, has long referred to Ben as the best criminal defense lawyer in the country.

When he and I met in 1987, Benjamin Brafman was in his late 30s, just starting his career as a defense lawyer, largely unknown in his profession and to the public alike. Ben's savvy was evident to me from day one, as was the detailed knowledge he brought to each "joint defense" prep session. Clearly, he had been doing his homework, and while the youngest lawyer in the room, was always a significant participant. I especially appreciated his sense of humor, something always important to me. He told jokes or humorous stories with ease; this was unsurprising in someone, as I was later to learn, who had originally wanted to be a professional comedian.

Ben's office was then in lower Manhattan, within walking distance of mine. We thus began our professional relationship and personal friendship. Back then, in the months that preceded the Ruggiero trial, I believed I had a good grasp of his abilities as a lawyer. Again, I did not know the half of it.

Once the trial started, I became increasingly impressed by Ben's performance as his talent began to dominate the proceedings, much to the delight of all defendants, who viewed him more and more as a key player in the overall defense. In multi-defendant trials you always want to be the lawyer who causes the jurors to move up in their seats as you rise to do your thing; Ben was emerging as just that lawyer. At the same time, other lawyers failed to please and were chastised by the clients accordingly. During an all-too memorable midmorning recess early in the trial, one of the lawyers for a minor defendant, upon losing a key motion to exclude certain evidence after making what can be charitably described as a lackluster legal argument, was pressed against the hall wall by one of the defendants, in plain view of all, and threatened. Another lawyer was completely barred from asking any more questions by his client, Johnny Carniglia, after a memorably horrible and completely unnecessary cross-examination, recreated below.

An FBI agent testified on direct examination to surveilling numerous meetings among certain of the defendants, as he outlined their various illegal activities to the jury. One of the more important meetings was held at a Brooklyn junkyard owned by defendant and alleged "made man," Johnny Carniglia (aka "Johnny Junkyard"). As related by the agent, the junkyard meeting was between one of the minor defendants and someone who would later become a government cooperator. Glaringly missing from the agent's narrative on direct examination was the presence or participation of the junkyard's owner, Johnny Carniglia.

On cross-examination, the lawyer for the defendant the government identified as the participant in the junkyard meeting did a nice job to minimize the damage and sat down. Unexpectedly, Carniglia's lawyer, Anthony Lombardino, then rose from his seat to cross-examine. Brafman and I exchanged anxious glances. What the hell was Lombardino doing? It is axiomatic to any experienced courtroom lawyer that once a favorable fact for your side has been established, you stay away from it like the plague until the "close of evidence" at the end of the trial, when it will be safe to use in summation.

There was no reason for Lombardino to get up. The witness was about to be excused without involving his client in anything. As a result, he would be able to argue that his client's absence from his own premises for this meeting showed he was uninvolved in any narcotics deal.

Turning his back on the gift he had been given, he recklessly (and unnecessarily) sought to stress his client's absence from the allegedly illegal activities. Lombardino pointed to his client and asked in a loud, dramatic voice, "You didn't see my client, Johnny Carniglia, there that day, did you?" The agent paused, looked over at the defense table and asked if Carniglia could please stand up, which Carniglia reluctantly did. At this point, anxiety at the defense table was at cardiac arrest levels. The agent then responded (and again, I am recreating the essence, not reproducing the exact words), "Now that I have a good look at him, I think, yes, he was there."

It was like a bomb had gone off.

Johnny Carniglia was viewed by law enforcement as a dangerous mobster, albeit, from my experience, one with both intelligence and a great sense of humor. He could barely contain his anger, because he, understandably, saw nothing funny about what had happened. After being confronted by Carniglia, Lombardino was not allowed to ask another question for weeks, and then only upon prior approval. From that point on, as directed by Gene Gotti, many of the cross-examinations were restricted to the handful of lawyers the clients trusted.

The pressure, day after day, week after week, month after month, of working in such an artificial and uncomfortable environment, including doing cross-examinations for clients who were not your own, was unbearable. Fischetti and Brafman carried much of the load of the extra assignments with apparent comfort. These assignments were really nerve-racking for me. It is hard enough to know all of your own client's vulnerabilities and strengths. You cannot possibly know everything you need to emphasize or avoid for someone you do not represent and hadn't spent months of preparation getting ready to defend. It was something I had never done before and would never have to do again. The Ruggiero trial was tension-packed enough even without these extra, dangerous cross-examinations. With them, it was nearly unbearable. You would not know it, however, by watching Ben Brafman.

The real "aha moment" came when a cooperating prosecution witness testified at length to a drug deal he claimed to have had with Ben's client, Mark Reiter (aka "Jew Boy"), an alleged "associate" of the Gambino family who dealt in drugs on the family's behalf. On direct examination the witness was shown a handwritten note made up of five words. One of the FBI agents who had surveilled a meeting between Reiter and the witness had previously described seeing a small piece of paper being passed from Reiter to the witness. The witness now identified that piece of paper as the note before him. He went on to explain to the jury how the five words on the note detailed a drug deal he had with Mark Reiter.

It was powerful testimony, as the note thus described, including weight and price, cried out "drug deal" and corroborated this witness's testimony in general. An important element of the RICO "enterprise" charged against all defendants seemed to be firmly in place.

When Ben got up to cross-examine there was, not surprisingly, a great deal of tension in the courtroom. That tension only increased when he slowly walked to the back of the courtroom and picked up an easel he had prepositioned against the rear wall. Fastened to the easel was a large, blank sheet of paper. Ben carried the easel into the well of the courtroom, and carefully placed it between himself and the witness at an angle that the jury could see it. (This was, of course, years before the electronic courtroom of today in which everything is done with computers and displayed on screens).

All of the dramatic stagecraft, the time-consuming, physical set-up of the cross-examination and what he was going to do with that set-up, created enormous pressure on success or failure. No one, myself included, had any idea what was next, but Ben had clearly put himself on a high wire without a net to catch him if he fell. With all eyes glued on him, Ben then took out a magic marker, and with it, took the witness through the note. One by one, in large, dark letters, he wrote each of the words from the note in the same relative location on the easel's sheet of paper.

After getting the witness to acknowledge that the easel's large sheet of paper now replicated the note he claimed described a drug deal with Mark Reiter, Ben focused on the five words, one at a time. With exquisite skill, he got the witness to admit that each word could also be a reference to aspects of a different drug deal the witness had been involved in with someone else. Ultimately, Ben got him to concede that, when read together, these same words even more accurately described the other drug deal, one unconnected to Mark Reiter or any of the other defendants on trial.

Poison had just been turned into caviar.

The combination of imagination, technique, incredible confidence, and an exhaustive knowledge of the underlying FBI reports detailing this witness's long career of crime provided to defense counsel under court rules just blew me away. I was impressed, relieved, grateful, and yes, jealous, all at the same time. He was Willie Mays, making plays in center field that a regular outfielder like myself, however seasoned and accomplished, could only aspire to.

The trial continued well beyond the initial two-month estimate.

This was in large measure because of the judge, Mark A. Costantino, who was generally regarded as the least qualified judge then sitting in the Eastern District of New York. Costantino was not only an underwhelming judicial figure, but he was also not the hardest worker. He often started the Ruggiero proceedings after 10:00 a.m., took long breaks during the day, and usually finished in the middle of the afternoon.

To provide some perspective, perhaps unfairly, contrast this with the work habits of Jack Weinstein, a judge on the same court before whom, as detailed earlier, I had my first trial as a prosecutor. Judge Weinstein sometimes conducted two trials concurrently. The first would begin at 8:00 a.m. There was perhaps one 20-minute break before the session ended at 1:00 p.m. At 1:30 p.m., the second trial would commence and go as long in the day as it took to reach a sensible stopping point, but rarely before 6:00 p.m. Judge Weinstein would have tried the Ruggiero case in six weeks or less. The average judge on the court would have kept within the original two-month estimate.

As the trial dragged on, from time to time Gene Gotti would invite some of the defense lawyers, always including his lawyer, Ron Fischetti, to have lunch with him and certain of the other defendants at the diner across the park bordering the Eastern District courthouse. It was an invitation that could not be declined. All of the defendants except Angelo Ruggiero (the only one incarcerated during the trial) answered to "Genie," and so their lawyers, like it or not, acted accordingly. For me it was a blessing, as I enjoyed a better relationship with Gene Gotti than I did with my own client.

Depending on what was then happening in the case, or which of the other defendants and lawyers were also part of the group, these sessions could be tense, they could be downright collegial, or both. To my surprise, Genie could be really funny. I was, however, always mindful that among my lunch companions were mobsters who were in constant warfare with gangland rivals. Any minute, gun-wielding hit men could come bursting through the door, heading for our table.

One such lunch session stands out. We were seated at a large, round table. I had my back to the diner's front door, and apparently without realizing it, kept looking over my shoulder. Gene Gotti noticed this and shouted out, "Hey, Katzberg, don't worry. The last thing you hear is the click." Everyone roared. "Don't worry, the last thing you hear is the click" became a punch line for Ron Fischetti, Ben Brafman, and me for decades thereafter whenever we found ourselves in a tough situation in one of our subsequent cases together.

There were also many moments of humor in the courtroom, a rarity in proceedings as serious as criminal trials. Usually the source was Judge Costantino, who, however unintentionally, provided one hilarious malapropism after another.

In one, a defense lawyer told the judge that a ruling he was about to make would not withstand scrutiny on appeal. Judge Costantino replied with something like, "I am not concerned. I am often reversed, but never for my rulings."

"Then for what, your ties?" Brafman whispered to me, as I watched Ron Fischetti lower his head so the judge would not be able see him laughing uncontrollably.

In another memorable Costantino gaff, I had raised a point of law with the judge about the expected testimony of the next government witness. I was met with a rambling, confused response. Seeking to focus the judge's attention on the specific point I had raised, I quoted the Federal Rule of Evidence that controlled the legal issue involved. In reply, Judge Costantino said, "I know that rule as well as I know your name, *Mr. Kapsburg.*" As I stood at the lectern, I could hear the lawyers and defendants behind me stifling laughter at the unintended butchering of my name.

Notwithstanding the occasional comic relief, by month three of the trial everyone was becoming increasingly irritable, lawyers and clients alike. Money problems only exacerbated the situation. In most criminal matters, the lawyers do not bill by the hour, but instead, charge flat fees. With the trial dragging on well beyond the two months originally anticipated, the lawyers, all of whom were solo practitioners or members of small firms, were getting crushed financially. Confined to the courtroom, they could not do any meaningful work for other clients to help pay the rent. The ongoing conversations between client and lawyer about additional legal fees added an extra level of tension and conflict.

My relationship with Eddie Lino continued to be problematic. Eddie tried to take advantage of every situation, including this one. He claimed his wife's bus company was in serious financial trouble and thus, no more money was available. I argued with him as much as one can argue with a reputed Mafia hit man. Realizing I needed help, I turned to Ron Fischetti. Ron spoke to Gene Gotti, who promised Ron that Eddie's wife would come through, which she ultimately did. This made Eddie even angrier and, as was obvious to all, our relationship deteriorated further. I never had anything remotely like the distrust and yes, fear, of a client before or since that I had with Eddie. It was a searing experience.

The trial finally ended in its fourth month, but not in the usual way. The FBI received evidence that associates of one of the defendants (I have forgotten which) had approached a juror in the case, potentially trying to influence him or her. A mistrial was declared.

Lino and I were each grateful to end the relationship.

The story ends later, in 1990.

I was at the train station, awaiting the early morning arrival of an AMTRAK train to Philadelphia, where I was to argue an appeal in a tax fraud case in the United States Court of Appeals for the Third Circuit. I saw plastered on the front page of the *New York Post* a grim photo of Eddie Lino lying face down in the street. The headline screamed of a gangland murder. Lino had been executed by two uniformed New York City police officers who had pulled over his big Mercedes sedan and then riddled it and him with bullets. It was reported that the corrupt cops had been hired by rival organized crime members to carry out the revenge killing.

Moments before the AMTRAK train pulled into the station, I was alerted by my office that Ben Brafman had called and urgently needed to speak with me. When I got Ben on the line, he asked, "So, *Mr. Kapsburg*, you got an alibi?"

James LaRossa

In the mid-1990s I had the great fortune of trying a two-defendant case in Brooklyn federal court with the late Jimmy LaRossa. Jimmy had been the first lawyer to beat me in the courtroom when I was a federal prosecutor (but alas, not the last) and was among the very best trial lawyers of his day. He had a high-profile clientele that included gangsters, labor leaders, celebrities, politicians, and Wall Street tycoons. Handsome, poised, and with a deep voice that resonated in the well of the courtroom, Jimmy had among the most successful boutique criminal defense practices in New York. Each time you try a case you learn something new (if you are paying attention), but working alongside Jimmy defending this particular case provided a master class.

To appreciate Jimmy's performance, a little background on cross-examination is necessary. Most people's impression of cross-examination comes from the media. While occasionally a realistic cross is presented, as for example in the movie classic, *Kramer vs. Kramer,* such instances are rare. Instead, the public is inundated with cartoonish portrayals in which, after just a few dramatic questions, a witness is brought to tears and admits to either trying to frame the defendant or to being the actual perpetrator. In real life, cross-examinations are pointed and tactical, not histrionic. The examiner employs a series of structured questions, strategically designed to either chip away at specific factual aspects of a witness's testimony, cast doubt on the character or credibility of the witness, or use the witness to make points helpful to the cross-examiner's cause.

There are many impediments to overcome in a cross-examination.

First, in all but the rarest circumstance, prosecution witnesses are not looking to help your cause. They are either openly hostile to your position or, at best, indifferent. With respect to FBI, IRS, and other governmental agent witnesses, they are not only hostile, but "professional witnesses," experienced in fending off cross-examination questions. Second, prosecutors spend hours rehearsing their witnesses' direct testimony, practicing the responses to questions they intend to ask in a predetermined sequence. Their rehearsal includes preparing the witnesses to fend off the questions likely to be asked on cross-examination. In sharp contrast, the cross-examiner in criminal trials is almost always face-to-face with the witness for the first time in the courtroom, without the benefit of any interpersonal preparation. You are trying to sing a duet with an unwilling partner who is reading from different sheet music.

With the deck thus stacked against you, it all comes down to judgment and control.

The threshold requirement is to accurately identify both what your examination can accomplish and the means by which to do so. You must thread the needle between aiming for too little and overreaching. The former diminishes the value of your cross, and the latter invites disaster.

Second, you have to accurately select the best of the case history and materials (prior statements, laboratory analyses, surveillance photos, emails, and the like) at your disposal to accomplish your goals.

Third, you have to execute by carefully laying the groundwork with a series of specific, preliminary questions, followed by more direct and narrow queries. You increasingly place the witness in a position where he or she cannot resist your direction and the result you seek without looking like a liar or a fool. All attempts by the witness to thwart or evade must be batted away, while the examiner, in full command of the facts, reflects the degree of anger or incredulity appropriate to the situation.

Finally, your questions must be structured within the limits imposed by the rules of evidence so your opponent (or the judge) has no basis to object and interfere. All this must be done in a coherent, compelling way that keeps the jury's attention.

The task can be daunting, especially given what is at stake in a criminal trial. Even in civil litigation, where it is money and not liberty on the line, the danger of embarrassing gaffes is omnipresent.

Years ago, *The Wall Street Journal* reported on a compilation made by the Massachusetts Bar Association of some of the "memorable questions" asked by its litigation members over the years. The list includes questions such as, "Are you qualified to give a urine sample?", "How far apart were the vehicles at the time of the collision?" and, "How many times have you committed suicide?" My favorite: "Q.: Doctor . . . is it possible that the patient was alive when you began your autopsy? A.: No. Q.: How can you be so sure? A.: "Because his brain was sitting on my desk in a jar."

In sharp contrast, as noted above, the cross-examination in *Kramer vs. Kramer* provides an example, however cinematically stylized, of a realistic, effective cross, albeit in the context of a civil, non-jury trial.

Mrs. Kramer, played by Meryl Streep, has sued her husband, played by Dustin Hoffman, for divorce and seeks custody of their young son, whom she abandoned years before. In her passionate direct testimony, Mrs. Kramer makes a compelling, emotional case to the court for her to be re-united with her son, stressing the importance of a successful mother-son relationship to her son's development. Howard Duff, as Mr. Kramer's lawyer, begins his cross-examination by having Mrs. Kramer admit just how faithful and devoted a husband and father Mr. Kramer has been. Once these facts supporting his client's maintaining custody are established, he then goes on to attack the thrust of her direct testimony, that is, that the child needs a full relationship with his mother and thus, she should be granted custody.

> Q. What was the longest personal relationship in your life outside of your parents and friends?
>
> A. I suppose it was my child.
>
> Q. Whom you were seeing twice a year.
>
> A. (No reply).
>
> Q. Mrs. Kramer, your husband, wasn't he the longest personal

relationship in your life?

A. (Nods her head).

Q. Speak up.

A. Yes.

Q. How long was that?

A. We were married a year before the baby and seven years after that.

Q. So you were a failure in the one, most important relationship in your life?

Opposing attorney: Objection.

Judge: Overruled. The witness's opinion on this is relevant.

A. I was not a failure.

Q. Oh, what do you call it then, a success? The marriage ended in a divorce.

A. I consider it less my failure than his.

Q. Congratulations, Mrs. Kramer, you've just rewritten matrimonial law. You were both divorced.

Opposing attorney: Objection.

Q. Your Honor, I would like to ask this model of civility and responsibility if she has ever succeeded at a relationship. Were you a failure at the most important relationship in your life?

A. It did not succeed.

Q. Not it, Mrs. Kramer, you. Were you a failure at the one, most important relationship in your life?

A. (Sobs).

The Court: Is that a yes?

Q. Nothing further, Your Honor.

In real life, while every good cross-examiner necessarily has his or her own style that reflects individual personalities and skill sets, there are some fundamental rules that apply. Although each rule has multiple exceptions, here is a basic, albeit selective, list.

Rule one: do not cross-examine a witness who did not hurt you on direct examination.

Anthony Lombardino's blatant violation of this basic rule in the Ruggiero trial, already described, is Exhibit A in support of this proposition. When the direct testimony of such a witness is over and the judge turns to you asking, "Any cross-examination?" it can be powerful to simply stand and announce, "No, questions, Your Honor." It sends a strong signal to the jury that nothing they just heard was important or harmful to your client. It also tells the jury that you are not there to waste time (something particularly precious to people taken away from family and work to sit on the case) and that you are not in love with the sound of your own voice.

Rule two: when you are hurt on direct examination, you must decide upon the theory of your cross.

Is the witness merely mistaken, or is he or she a liar? It is hard to be both. If the former, your approach is tempered as you bring out facts to demonstrate the error. For example, you may be able to challenge whether the witness had an adequate opportunity to observe the events to which he or she testified, or show he or she was absent from other important events that impact what was claimed in direct testimony. If a liar, you go after that person with indignation and disbelief in what is called a "destructive cross."

Finally, the opposite of the destructive cross is a "constructive cross," one in which you make the witness your own, for at least part of the examination.

In this situation, and an exception to the first rule, the witness has knowledge of other things beyond his or her direct testimony, things helpful to your case. After touching on what was covered on direct to the degree required, the cross-examiner, in a more positive mode, brings out these new matters, essentially making the government's witness his or her own. The order can be reversed, as in the *Kramer vs. Kramer* cross quoted above, in which the cross-examiner first establishes his client's exemplary personal history and stability before attacking the witness for lacking same. The best constructive cross-examinations make your opponent sorry to have called the witness in the first place. In my experience, some of the most adroit cross-examiners I have seen excel at destroying a witness, but fall short on knowing how and when to do a constructive cross.

All of which brings us back to Jimmy LaRossa.

In our trial, he simply destroyed a coconspirator who testified to various transactions with his client and mine. He confronted the witness with previous statements that were either in whole or in part different than what was said on direct. Talk about control. Again, I do not have a transcript, so what follows is my best attempt to recreate what occurred as accurately as possible.

From the moment he stepped up to the lectern, there was no question who was in charge. Jimmy slowly took off his glasses, held them in his hand, leaned on the lectern, and in his deep, baritone voice, began the way he began every cross. "Good morning, Mr. _____, my name is LaRossa, James LaRossa, and I represent Mr.

_____." He then immediately seized on an offhand remark volun-
teered by the witness near the end of his direct testimony. "I want to
start with something you said just a few moments ago." The remark
Jimmy was highlighting came in response to questions asked by the
prosecutor that enabled the witness to briefly recount and explain his
long, prior criminal record. "Bringing it out on direct," as it is often
called, is a standard prosecutorial tactic employed to take the sting
out of a potential cross-examination of a witness's unsavory past
by acknowledging it on direct. All good cross-examiners pay strict
attention during the direct and take copious notes. This is because
sometimes, as in this case, a witness can unintentionally give you
an unexpected gift, seemingly telling the cross-examiner, "Here is
my head. I do not need it anymore. Please sever it from my body."

The trick is to recognize the gift and then make the most
of it, which is just what Jimmy did. Again, I am reconstructing
from memory.

Seeking to first "lock it in," Jimmy held up his yellow legal pad,
put his glasses back on, and read from the pad. "My notes indicate
that you said, 'My rap sheet [official criminal record] makes me look
much worse than I really am.' Did I get that right?" The witness
hesitated and replied that he said, "something like that." "Something
like that? How about exactly that?" Jimmy asked. Again, the witness
demurred. LaRossa would have none of it. "Do you want me to ask
the court reporter to read back exactly what you said?" Faced with
that unpleasant prospect, the witness acknowledged those were his
precise words.

Jimmy then took the witness through each prior crime as entered on his "rap sheet." Following each entry, such as "assault in
the second degree," LaRossa went into the gory details of what
the witness had actually done, activity far more gruesome than the

lesser crimes to which he ultimately pleaded. He concluded each by asking the witness whether when he told the jury his rap sheet made him look worse than he was whether he had those details in mind. There was, of course, no answer that he could give, so some were "no," and others "yes." Realizing what he was up against, the witness offered little resistance to the onslaught that followed.

What struck me was Jimmy's ability to recognize the power of a seemingly off-hand, "throwaway" remark that most lawyers would not have even noticed, and his spontaneous and devastating ability to turn the "throwaway" into a sledgehammer that crippled his adversary even before he got to his prepared material. Inexperienced lawyers tend to be glued to their predetermined cross-examination outline, and even if they recognize an unexpected opening in the direct, lack the talent and confidence to go off script and exploit a new opportunity. Jimmy not only took advantage of the "throwaway" remark, but took control. With his victim already on the ropes, Jimmy drove home his planned cross with perfect levels of alternating sarcasm and anger in his voice, an unmistakable tempo to the back and forth, and a dramatic cadence that drew everyone in, especially the jurors.

LaRossa reduced a witness who seemed so steady on direct into an unwilling partner in his own destruction, as he was forced to confront all of the contradictions and falsehoods that undermined his credibility. And like any great performer, LaRossa saved the most impactful impeachment, about a lie the witness told in the grand jury that indicted the case, for a dramatic finish. When he finally turned to the judge and in a respectful tone announced, "No further questions," the jurors moved back from the edge of their seats. The witness just sagged in his.

Days later, when an FBI agent took the stand, Jimmy switched from destruction to construction. Using multiple "302 Reports" this agent and others in his group had written about the overall investigation, Jimmy brought out one detail after another tending to show that his client's role in the events at issue were different than the theory of the government's case. Variations of "I am correct, am I not, that your investigation revealed [a specific fact]" were each followed by the witness' often reluctant acknowledgement that it was so. While a new, different rhythm had emerged, one with a more respectful and constructive tone, the performance was nonetheless compelling, once again capturing the attention of each and every member of the jury. The end result was the trial record now contained new, helpful details that would not have emerged without the cross.

During the recess that followed, I joked to Jimmy that he did more testifying than the agent. Jimmy looked at me seriously, assuming the mentor role he often adopted with younger lawyers, and said, "I testify all the time, in every way I can. I testify in how I dress and how I speak to the judge. I even testify in how I take off my fucking glasses. That's what good lawyers do."

It was a wonderful experience for me, notwithstanding the ultimate result. The jury convicted both of our clients on all counts.

Patrick Tuite

Back in 1983, Dennis Berkson, a law school friend who had become a successful criminal defense lawyer in Chicago, contacted me and asked if I would represent a colleague of his, Richard Joseph. Richard was a Chicago real estate lawyer who had just been indicted in federal court in Springfield, Illinois, along with a somewhat notorious Chicago criminal defense attorney, Marvin Glass. They were charged with a conspiracy to "structure" cash transactions, so as to avoid then-recently enacted currency reporting obligations imposed on financial institutions.

The currency reporting regulations were initially intended as a weapon in the "war on drugs." These federal statutes require the reporting of any single cash deposit or withdrawal of $10,000 or more to the IRS. Attempts to avoid the reporting requirements by "structuring" the cash transactions, that is, breaking them up into multiple deposits or withdrawals of lesser sums that totaled $10,000 or more, was made a federal crime. Glass and Joseph were charged with conspiring to do just that.

Marvin Glass had represented a young married couple, who from all outer appearances, were attractive, clean-cut Midwesterners. Appearances aside, they were major marijuana dealers who shipped their product across the nation in tractor trailers. Glass had referred them to Richard Joseph, a real estate solo practitioner who rented an office in his suite, to represent them in the purchase of a home in New England. The couple would regularly bring Richard smallish amounts of cash, which he dutifully deposited into his attorney's trust account. The account eventually contained the full six-figure purchase price, which was wired to the seller's bank to complete the purchase.

Joseph insisted he did not know that the currency was the proceeds of the young couple's marijuana business. Whatever doubts one might have had about his naïveté made no difference. It seemed to be a triable case.

In referring the matter to me, Dennis mentioned that Marvin Glass had hired one of Chicago's best criminal defense attorneys, Pat Tuite, and that I would enjoy working with Pat. Notwithstanding my respect for Dennis, I took a wait-and-see approach, given my prior dealings with attorneys who failed to live up to big reputations. With Pat, it did not take long to see why *The Chicago Lawyer* named him the very best of the city's criminal defense attorneys. Just as important, Pat was always respectful and appropriate, never letting ego get in the way.

The trial judge was Middle District of Illinois Chief Judge Waldo Ackerman, a gracious, seasoned, and well-prepared jurist who was a treat to work before. More than once he expressed his pleasure in having "good lawyers from out of town" work before him, and gave us freedom to "do our thing" throughout. Given that Marvin Glass was the principal defendant, against whom the majority of evidence existed, and in light of his extraordinary skill set, Pat's voice dominated the defense performance, while I mostly sang in harmony.

In my complementary role I felt less overall pressure, and when from time to time I was out front, was even better able to execute. As in the previously discussed extortion trial before Judge Schwartz, too often in the past I had been unable to limit the role of less skilled lawyers representing less significant co-defendants with whom I found myself on trial. Whether it was their ego or ignorance that got in the way did not matter. Their failure to understand the limits of their proper role and/or talents became an impediment not only to what I was trying to do, but to a successful defense of their own client. Surely, Pat Tuite was even more frequently confronted with this problem than I. Given my ready acceptance of our respective roles, Pat and I got along wonderfully well, coordinated our efforts with no difficulty, and ended up getting both clients acquitted.

Good lawyers learn from each other and try to incorporate what they see in others into their own tool kit. You take something someone else does that works for him or her and use it yourself in a subsequent trial. You fit it to the facts or circumstances of the case and adapt it to reflect your own personality and style. If it works, you keep it in your arsenal. If not, you discard it. I picked up a number of new tricks from Pat and adapted them to my own use.

For example, I loved how he crafted his opening remarks to the jury in such a way as to be able to refer back to them in his summation at the close of the case, and basically say, "told you so." I never tried another case again without doing the same type of thing, but in my own way. I thereafter began every summation with some version of, "Ladies and gentlemen, I want to start this summation, which is my last opportunity to address you directly, by referring back to what I said to you in my first opportunity to address you when this trial began, that is, in my opening statement." From there I would segue into what I had either predicted in my opening they would hear during the trial, or problems with the government's case that I had red flagged.

In addition, I outright stole a portion of his summation in the Glass and Joseph trial, reconstructed below, and used it as a key part of one of the best summations I have ever given.

In her trial summation, the prosecutor kept harping on Marvin Glass's role as a criminal defense attorney who represented drug dealers. This was not an insignificant or unfair point; how could he not have known the money his drug-dealing clients had given to Richard Joseph to deposit was not from narcotics? But she seemed to be going a bit further, trying to tarnish Glass' character with the jury simply because he represented drug dealers.

Whether the character attack was inadvertent or intentional I will never know, but in either event, it was a mistake. Pat's summation jumped all over it. Unfortunately, I do not have a transcript of the trial. I cannot recreate in these pages the dazzling verbiage, his powerful delivery, or its dramatic impact, but will try to convey the essence of his summation as best as I can below.

> Ladies and gentlemen, Ms. _____ has made much of the fact that my client, Marvin Glass, is a criminal lawyer. A lawyer who defends drug dealers. Why so much emphasis on a basic fact that is not in dispute? Is it because, in and of itself, that proves anything, or is it because she wants to prejudice you against him? I cannot say. But what I will say, and will say in the strongest terms, is this. Marvin Glass and I are both proud to be lawyers who defend our fellow citizens accused of crimes. There are many wonderful trades and professions in our great country—doctors, teachers, sales persons [he actually recited the professions of the jurors based on our notes in the jury selection process], but there is only one, only one profession that is so fundamentally important to our democracy, that it is etched in the United States Constitution as the only non-governmental profession guaranteed by our forefathers as a constitutional right—lawyers who represent people charged with crimes.

It was brilliant. I am convinced to this day that if Pat had not taken this negativity about criminal lawyers out of the case in the dramatic and compelling way he did, and wrapped his client in the warm protective blanket of his own authority and class, Marvin Glass would have been convicted.

CHAPTER TEN

ROAD GAMES

While the core of our practice at Kaplan & Katzberg was in New York City—with two important and busy federal district courts, the Southern and Eastern Districts of New York, separated by the Brooklyn Bridge—I also represented clients all over the country. Six of these matters ultimately resulted in trials, three federal and three state, which took me to Newark, New Jersey; Tampa, Florida; Springfield, Illinois; Indianapolis, Indiana; Winston-Salem, North Carolina; and Memphis, Tennessee.

Trying cases away from home presented more than a few logistical issues, such as hotel accommodations, finding and coordinating with local counsel, obtaining office space, and the like. These issues rarely became problematic. On the professional front, I was fortunate to have strong backup at my firm to cover for me in the interim with other client matters. At home, my wife, Leslie, handled the multiplicity of issues our three children had with their father being away for weeks, sometimes more than a month, at a time. As a result, I was pretty much free to get into an appropriate, battle-oriented mindset on these trips.

Significant to the "road game" experience, at least for me, was the "hired gunslinger" mentality. As already noted, in defending any criminal case, particularly in federal court, you are always the underdog. Notwithstanding this reality, trial lawyers like the ones described in this book, and even those not on that elite level, create a kind of self-serving mythology. When it comes to the ultimate outcome of any trial, it is I, not the judge with life tenure and complete authority over everything that occurs, or the prosecutor with the U.S. Treasury and the FBI or IRS at his or her disposal, who will have the greatest impact. Like the baseball player who is confident of getting a hit every time he enters the batter's box, despite knowing that even the greatest hitters in the history of the game fail to do so more than two out of every three chances, this mentality is necessary for any degree of success.

I found this mindset especially important in trials out of state, particularly in areas of the country where I stood out as an outsider, a reality that only magnified my underdog status. Again, the effective trial lawyer is able to connect with jurors, allowing them to relate to you and what you are trying to get across. Any gap, whether cultural, ethnic, religious, or class, becomes a potential impediment to success. While I had less concern in the Newark or Tampa trials, in the Winston-Salem and Memphis trials, to varying degrees, being an outsider was an issue.

The Memphis case contained elements that made my "outsider status" a particular problem.

Mark Singer had been a successful financial advisor in Philadelphia, Pennsylvania. Among his clients was a man named Clayton Smart. Smart and a fellow Oklahoman, Steven Smith, had purchased cemeteries in three states, including one in Memphis, Tennessee. Smart then sold prepaid cemetery plots, along with related funeral services, to people looking to finalize such arrangements and take that part of the future burden of their death off family members. The money they paid was deposited into a discrete trust fund to ensure availability when, sometimes many years later, the funeral was to take place. Singer, as financial advisor for the investments in all three states, received fees totaling some $1.3 million.

As it turns out, Smart and Smith allegedly stole most of the trust money, to the tune of some $22 million. They and Singer were charged in Memphis, Tennessee, and Indianapolis, Indiana, with state criminal offenses, including conspiracy, money laundering, and theft. Investigations in the third state, Michigan, were also under way. The cases generated sensational publicity in each city, as people were unable to bury next of kin because the money the deceased paid for his or her burial had been looted.

I was retained by Mark to replace his original attorney after that attorney had been unable to work out a "global disposition" to satisfy all three states. Such a disposition would have allowed Singer to make peace with all three jurisdictions, serve only one (hopefully limited) jail term, pay whatever fines could be agreed upon, and get it all behind him. Winning once is hard enough. Winning three times is virtually impossible, especially since each successive prosecution benefits from the experiences, both good and bad, of the prior trial. Yet, I was brought in to try these cases because there was no other option.

My initial meeting with prosecutors in Memphis only confirmed the lack of alternatives. They expressed great confidence in their evidence and took a very hard line, insisting on a guilty plea exposing Singer to ten years in jail. It was clear to me I would do no better than my predecessor in working out a satisfactory disposition short of trial, and so I set my mind to get ready for battle.

In going through the evidence received in discovery, I concluded that the Indianapolis case against Mark was the stronger of the
two. The biggest issue for Memphis was whether Clayton Smart
would work out a deal with local prosecutors and testify. While
having a co-defendant cooperate and testify against you was usually
very harmful, in this case, I hoped for it. My ability to blame it all
on Clayton Smart would be greatly increased if I could make him
the face of the prosecution, cross-examine him before the jury, and
expose him as the fraudster I believed him to be. On the other hand,
if he would be defending the case alongside us in the courtroom,
that road would be a lot more difficult.

It did not take long for our strategy to emerge: try Memphis
first, somehow win, or at least get a hung jury, and then negotiate
a far better "global" deal than previously available. As a result of
certain steps we took, which need not be detailed here, and luck
(as much of the latter as the former), we got to try Memphis first.
Mark Singer was the only defendant on trial.

Further to the "outsider" issue, and in addition to being concerned with the inflammatory nature of the underlying crime, I was
painfully aware of the potential resistance we faced from jurors who
might have a difficult time relating to me and my client. Here I was,
a Jewish lawyer from New York, with my Asian associate, Bryan Ha.
We were defending a Jewish "Wall Street" guy from Philadelphia,
who was charged with making more than $1 million helping a client
of his scam poor people in Memphis out of their right to a decent
burial. I had no idea how I was going to handle that.

We caught a break with the judge, W. Otis Higgs, an ordained
Christian Methodist Episcopal Minister, long-time civil rights advocate, and twice unsuccessful candidate for mayor. When he died in
2013, Judge Higgs was hailed in the Memphis media as a "gracious

giant," a description fully consistent with my experience in his courtroom. We got along wonderfully well. He called me "the big city
lawyer," and seemed to enjoy watching me work. Conferences with
the lawyers in his chambers were especially pleasurable, as Judge
Higgs sprinkled most of these discussions with his folksy sense of
humor and great storytelling ability, unsurprising in a man who
delivered sermons every Sunday. His chamber's walls were covered
with enlarged photos of the judge with Martin Luther King, Jr. and
other civil rights leaders, and he shared his reminiscences of them
when prompted either by me or one of the prosecutors.

By this time in my career my trial performances followed a
set pattern. As previously noted, in my opening statement to the
jury before the prosecution called its first witness, I would, in essence, make a deal with jurors. I would predict specific things they
would hear or come to learn during the course of the trial. The tacit
agreement was that if the evidence turned out the way I predicted
it would, I would be entitled to ask them to acquit my client. If it
did not, no such request could be justified.

During the trial, I would focus on the things I opened on, highlighting them whenever possible. In summation, after all of the
evidence was presented, I would refer back to what was predicted
in the opening, detail how the evidence was just as I had promised,
and basically say, "I have lived up to my part of the bargain, now it
is your turn."

Summing up, as it is called, is the ultimate moment, the time to
spend all of the personal capital you have (hopefully) accumulated
with the jury from day one. It is when everything you worked so
hard to accomplish during the trial is organized and presented in the
most compelling way possible, so as to convince 12 strangers to see
things your way. My summations used a variation of a structural

approach I learned from other defense lawyers long ago, combined with a courtroom adaptation of lessons learned from William A. Behl, my brilliant speech and debate professor at Brooklyn College. He taught that in giving a "speech to persuade" (the epitome of which would be a summation) you "tell them what you are going to tell them, tell them, then tell them you told them." In essence, I viewed the entire trial as a "speech to persuade."

I opened to the Singer jury by predicting the state would call witnesses who had been lied to by Clayton Smart, people who had assisted Smart's schemes because they believed those lies. I promised to establish Smart's falsehoods one after the other. I went on to predict that the evidence would show among those deceived was Mark Singer. Finally, I predicted that certain of the state's witnesses would lie to them in this trial in order to cover up how they allowed Smart to use and deceive them. I also said the prosecution would be calling these people as witnesses even though they have to have known that their testimony would be questionable at best.

Normally, such predictions would be dangerous indeed, as one's ability to demonstrate actual lies told to, or by, multiple key witnesses, no matter how strong a cross-examiner you might be, would be "iffy." In this case, however, there was a great deal of "gold" in the discovery material, giving me the wherewithal to deliver on my promises. Under these circumstances, especially with the compelling need to deflect the enormous prejudice inherent in the sensational charges themselves, I felt comfortable with the risk.

My comfort level only increased as I gauged the reaction of three young, male members of the jury. The Tennessee jury selection process was much like that in New York State courts, that is, the lawyers conduct the *voir dire* to a significant extent. My individual interchanges with these men went well, and I was relieved they each survived the selection process. While the other jurors seemed to be listening to my opening remarks with varying degrees of interest, the three men, now seated near each other, seemed to be particularly attentive when I predicted the state would be calling known liars to the stand and I promised to expose them.

I made sure to focus on the trio as much as possible as the trial progressed.

The trial began painfully, with victims of the fraud presenting truly awful tales of not being able to bury loved ones, even though meaningful sums had been paid years prior into a trust the family believed had secured the future. One particularly horrible story remains with me. A municipal worker whose mother passed away and who could not be buried in the Memphis cemetery plot she had paid for, was forced to drive his deceased mother's corpse in his truck to a cemetery and funeral home operated by a distant relative in Waco, Texas. How do you cross-examine that? You don't. I simply expressed sorrow for his loss and announced that I had no questions.

Once we got through these opening witnesses, the trial went well, as the materials I had in hand to establish a myriad of false-hoods proved to be as potent as I had hoped.

The prosecutors called too many witnesses, allowing me to establish additional falsehoods and evasions. It is always a tough call for prosecutors to figure out how much evidence is enough. After investigating a matter fully, and carefully preparing your case over time, the last thing you want to do is leave any meaningful evidence unpresented to the jury. On the other hand, you do not want to bury the gold with base metals. I believed the Memphis prosecution team erred on the side of too much, and in "over-trying" their case, gave me more of a fighting chance than I would have otherwise had.

One witness not called was Clayton Smart. Whether he was

available as a cooperator and prosecutors were prudent enough not to call him, or he hadn't made a deal and was thus unavailable to them, I did not know. At any rate, by the time summations rolled around, I felt we had a shot, especially as I continued to feel good about the apparent reaction of the same three male jurors to some of my cross-examinations. Given the inherently inflammatory nature of the charges, however, and my being an obvious "outsider," there was plenty of room for concern.

Fortunately, the prosecutor's initial summation provided an opening to at least deal with my "outsider" status.

In the state of Tennessee, just as in the federal courts, because they have the burden of proof, prosecutors give two summations. The first is an initial, full, summation of their case and the second is a shorter, "rebuttal" summation, limited to answering issues raised in the defense summation occurring between the two. While going twice gives a decided advantage to prosecutors, I learned over time that with some luck, I could use this structure to my advantage. To do so fully requires three things.

The first is a mistake by the prosecutor in his or her initial remarks that creates an opening.

The second is coming up with a way to exploit the mistake or take full advantage of that opening, and inserting that "piece" in the appropriate place in the outline of my prepared remarks.

And the third, based upon what the prosecutor has already said, or more typically what the prosecutor has avoided in the initial summation, is to raise one or two additional questions that I was confident my opponent could not satisfactorily answer. I would then challenge the prosecutor to answer these questions in rebuttal, and propose that unless they were answered to the jurors' full satisfaction, the prosecutor had no right to ask them to convict.

Further, I would tell the jury that if the prosecutor avoids addressing these questions, that means he or she has no good answer. This strategy has the effect of potentially enabling me to shape the prosecutor's rebuttal remarks, and thus help direct the jury's consideration of my client's fate around the factual issues I have chosen.

In the Memphis trial, the prosecutor's summation gave me an unexpected opening to deal with the "outsider" issue. Again, I do not have the transcript, so the following "quotes" are rough approximations from memory. During the initial summation, which was otherwise quite good, the prosecutor described me more than once as "my friend from New York." In my summation I referred to that description and asked why that was necessary. "Did he think you couldn't tell?" Building on the smiles and laughter that followed, I went on. "What does the fact that I am from New York have to do with the evidence against Mark Singer? Was Mr. ___ appealing to your view of the evidence, or was he appealing to something else? And if he was appealing to something else, what does that say about the confidence he has in the actual evidence against Mark Singer?"

Jury deliberations were extended. The jurors sent notes to Judge Higgs in the first few days asking for additional instructions on the law. Days of silence were followed by notes in which the jury reported difficulty in reaching a unanimous verdict on any of the counts in the indictment. Instructions to continue deliberating were followed by silence.

I tried to use the long days of deliberation to get around Memphis a little. While I learned that ordering ribs at a restaurant required you to decide whether you wanted them "wet" or "dry" ("wet" with gobs of barbeque sauce, please), and found a not-too touristy blues club to enjoy, I continued to feel very much the outsider from New York.

I noticed that when going to or coming from court, walking the streets of Memphis dressed in my courtroom attire, I stood out to a particular segment of the population. White men and women of all races pretty much ignored me, but black men of any age almost always tried to make eye contact. At first I was confused, but soon realized that they recognized me as an outsider, and one with perhaps more wealth or status. All they were seeking was my recognition of them, that we inhabited the same world.

This conclusion was reinforced by a weekend visit to the National Civil Rights Museum. Dr. King had come to Memphis, the city of his assassination, to support a sanitation workers strike. The museum featured pictures of the black strikers on the march, all carrying signs that said, "I am a Man." That's what these black men were silently, and perhaps unconsciously, communicating and asking me to confirm on the streets of Memphis. It hurt to realize that decades after the King assassination there were still places where the need for basic respect had still not been fulfilled. It made me even more anxious to be home.

The jury eventually reported that, despite their best and repeated efforts, they could not reach a unanimous verdict, as three of its members steadfastly refused to convict. I could never be certain who the holdouts were, but I had a strong guess. Judge Higgs declared a mistrial, and Bryan Ha and I raced to the airport to catch the first plane back to New York. It was many months before I would again eat ribs.

Mark Singer was ultimately convicted after trial the next year in Indianapolis. We eventually made a global deal. He was sentenced to two years in jail on the Indiana charges, such time to be served "concurrently" to satisfy charges in Memphis to which he pleaded guilty. Michigan never brought charges.

CHAPTER ELEVEN
JUDGING THE JUDGES

Federal judges impact our existence in virtually every sphere imaginable. Especially on the Supreme Court and circuit court levels, these men and women, who are appointed for life, make decisions that meaningfully affect individual liberties, voting rights, abortion rights, free speech, commercial rights, religious freedom, and a host of other rights and privileges too long to detail.

Most of the general public either takes these extraordinary powers for granted, or remains substantially unaware of them, and is blissfully under-informed about the individuals who wield that enormous power. The public's ignorance of the Supreme Court is well documented. For example, respected surveys have shown that only 43 percent of those polled could name a single member of the High Court, and only one in three correctly stated (or guessed) the number of female Supreme Court Justices. Given the degree of public ignorance about the Supreme Court, one shudders to imagine the paucity of knowledge concerning our circuit courts, their role in our democracy, or the individual appellate judges who have such meaningful power over our lives.

It is hardly surprising, therefore, that there exist so many false-hoods, platitudes, and caricatures about the federal judiciary.

A common description of judges places them in the role of baseball umpires simply calling balls and strikes. This is how Milton Gould, the "lawyer's lawyer" referenced in Chapter Five, described judges in his rejoinder to my then-boss, Chief Assistant United States Attorney Ed Korman. Milton used the umpire analogy to minimize the significance of judges and their role from the perspective of an All-Star baseball player. After all, the fans show up (and pay for their tickets) to see the players, not the men in blue.

More problematic, the umpire analogy has often been used as a facile way to avoid scrutiny of personal beliefs that necessarily have an impact on eventual jurisprudential analysis and decisions. A well-known invocation of the umpire analogy as dodge came from John Roberts, now the Chief Justice of the Supreme Court, at his U.S. Senate confirmation hearing. Roberts, promising to merely call balls and strikes, used the umpire analogy to sidestep key questions of his judicial views and outlook on important subjects such as abortion rights.

Sadly, displaying an ignorance of both baseball and judging (or perhaps reflecting the view that the nominee would surely be confirmed no matter what the inquiry), the senators let him get away with it. I wish one of the senators would have reminded Chief Justice to be Roberts that, as is well-known to every serious base-ball fan, there are home plate umpires that pitchers much prefer compared to batters, and home plate umpires that batters much prefer compared to pitchers. The difference? Their view of the strike zone. Some umpires have a broader view, calling pitches that are somewhat higher, lower, more outside, or more inside home plate as strikes, while others take a more restrictive approach. Hitters obviously prefer a narrower strike zone and pitchers a more expanded zone. As a consequence, how the game is played and how it turns out, can be materially influenced by which umpire stands behind home plate. Thus, follow-up questions for the Chief Justice to be that focused on his "judicial strike zone" might have provided a more enlightened discourse.

Even a full discourse on judicial philosophy can ignore key aspects of a particular judge's perspective that will surely impact his or her rulings.

The late Justice Antonin Scalia was a leading proponent of the so-called "textualist methodology" and its philosophical brother, "originalism," which has greatly impacted legal analysis on all sides of the judicial spectrum over the past several decades. In essence, "textualists/originalists" seek to analyze a given constitutional provision or statute based upon how a reasonable reader of that text would have understood it at the time it was written. As a result, the role of otherwise important things such as the intention of the drafters of the text at issue (usually referred to as legislative intent), or the policy consequences of a "textual" interpretation on today's world, are either eliminated from consideration or have greatly reduced significance.

The ultimate consequence is that judicial discretion, on the conscious level, at least, is supposed to be greatly limited.

A meaningful analysis of "textualism/originalism" is well beyond both my scholarly capabilities and the purposes of this book. It does seem odd to me, however, that a theory of Constitutional interpretation that limits consideration to the actual words and the meaning of those words at the time they were written, is not based on a direction that is actually in the Constitution. Most importantly, even if we accept the problematic premise that a twenty-first century judge has the ability to put himself or herself into the mindset of a reader who lived many decades or centuries in the past, who with respect to the Constitution, was a white man who likely owned slaves, that does not end the inquiry. Are we to believe that the individual "textualist/originalist" judge's personal views and life experiences will nonetheless not play a role in the decision-making process, consciously or otherwise? Is it conceivable that Justice Scalia, a devout Roman Catholic who firmly believed in the existence of the Devil, was somehow able to divorce himself from his innermost, life-long beliefs when he considered the cases before him? A recent opinion piece by Georgia State University law professor Eric J. Segall examines certain opinions of Supreme Court "originalists" and concludes that the label is merely "cover for imposing conservative value judgments."

While much of the criticism of philosophical labels has been directed to conservatives, there has been abundant opprobrium directed at other parts of the spectrum as well. For example, the outspoken Judge Richard Posner, now retired from the Seventh Circuit Court of Appeals after serving some four decades, described his judicial philosophy this way: "I pay little attention to legal rules, statutes, constitutional provisions. A case is just a dispute. The first thing you ask yourself—forget the law—what is a sensible resolution of the dispute?" But, what about precedent? "When you have a Supreme Court case or something similar, they're often extremely easy to get around." Unsurprisingly, Judge Posner's critics have called him "lawless."

What is largely missing in the back and forth is a basic fact that cannot be ignored. Judges, like all human beings, are products of their individual life experiences. By definition, this covers the entire spectrum of judges, whatever their professed judicial theology. As

Linda Greenhouse, the brilliant constitutional scholar and *New York Times* Supreme Court contributing opinion writer, observed:

> Judges, like anyone else, come equipped with basic assumptions about how the world works. Those assumptions have consequences. Justice Sotomayor learned about the criminal justice system on the ground as a young prosecutor in the Manhattan district attorney's office and came away with a fine eye for everything that can go wrong in a criminal case. The only other former prosecutor on the Supreme Court, Justice Samuel Alito Jr., was the top federal prosecutor in New Jersey, and from that rather elevated vantage point evidently concluded that the criminal justice system works quite well most of the time. It's hardly surprising that Justice Sotomayor votes frequently to set convictions aside, while Justice Alito almost never does.

The judge as umpire analogy is, in my view, even less apt when describing judges on the trial level, where I lived my professional life for over four decades.

It is in the trial courts where a popular old dictum is most visibly true: "the law is not what it says, but what it does." There is less need on the trial level for complex statutory interpretation, and the rules provide judges with a good deal of discretion. The focus in the district courts is on utilizing the applicable federal rules and exercising that discretion to provide fair and expeditious decision-making in the legal disputes that are before the court. District Judges must make these often-difficult judgments without benefit of hindsight available to a reviewing court. Most importantly, they must do so while dealing directly with the human beings who face the real-life consequences of the outcome.

Appellate judges do not regularly read the painful, heartfelt letters written by the victims of the person they are about to sentence; they do not have to hear the pleas of family members whose lives will be destroyed if the man or woman they are sentencing goes to jail. Indeed, appellate judges almost never deal with the actual parties involved in the underlying matter, be it civil or criminal. While it can be argued that insularity from such potentially emotional triggers is necessary for appellate judges to more "objectively" rule on the matters before them, being disconnected from the real world is rarely, if ever, a completely good thing. However "intellectually pure" they may be, judges must be able to connect with the real-world consequences of their rulings.

Day in and day out, district court judges must exercise their discretion to "do the right thing" for actual human beings appearing before them. This often involves the little things that are never noticed by the general public—or indeed, by an appellate panel reviewing their work—because they are rarely part of what is challenged on appeal.

An example. During my tenure as a federal prosecutor in Brooklyn, in addition to the venerated Jack B. Weinstein, already discussed, the Eastern District bench had two of the most substantial human beings I have ever encountered, John Dooling and Orrin Judd. Each reflected an almost godly combination of wisdom and humanity that one very rarely encounters in or out of the courtroom. I never had the privilege of actually trying a case before Judge Dooling, but I was lucky enough to try two cases before Judge Judd. To me, his courtroom was a cathedral of the law. Orrin Judd was a deeply religious man, with an impressive scholarly background, having graduated from Harvard Law School with top honors. He then served as a law clerk to the esteemed Second Circuit Judge Learned Hand. An analogous scientific equivalent would be having studied the theory of relatively under Einstein.

By the time I had my first trial before Judge Judd, I already had some experience under my belt and was thus able to be relatively relaxed enough to appreciate the experience. The case was run-of-the-mill, as was my adversary. There was one piece of evidence, very impactful evidence, that under the Federal Rules of Evidence, Judge Judd had properly excluded from the government's case before the trial began, as overly prejudicial to the defendant.

In my direct examination of one of the government witnesses, I took him through all of his testimony, but stopped just short of the precluded area. On cross-examination my opponent foolishly entered the forbidden zone, asking questions about one of its aspects. On redirect examination I began to explore the full, damaging material. My opponent quickly objected and asked for a sidebar with the judge.

At sidebar, my opponent cited the pre-trial ruling of preclusion. I replied that I had carefully avoided the area on direct, but since my opponent went into it to a material degree on cross-examination, he had "opened the door" to my full exploration. Under controlling case law, when a party who successfully moves to preclude certain evidence actually introduces it himself in some way, the other party has the right to use that evidence because the first party "opened the door." Judge Judd looked down at me and said, "Mr. Katzberg, I certainly agree that as a matter of law the door has been opened, but as a matter of fairness, I just cannot let you walk through it."

Orrin Judd was, in effect, protecting the defendant against the ineptitude of his own lawyer. Most judges would have upheld my correct legal position and allowed me to do real damage, all without fear of reversal on appeal. But Orrin Judd was not like most judges. I lost the ruling, but my admiration for the man who put fairness above the literal imposition of the rules only increased. The defendant was ultimately convicted, but only after Orrin Judd made damn sure his trial met the highest standards of due process.

Taken as a whole, the federal judiciary is comprised of among the most intelligent and qualified attorneys you can find. Of course, some are surely not at or even near that level, and never would have made it, say, as a lawyer in private practice, let alone be qualified for the federal judiciary. Many others are the elite of the profession, and have forsaken lucrative careers in private practice for public service.

All federal judges enter into a sort of priesthood. On the public level, for example, federal judges assiduously stay away from political activity. In private life, they try to stay clear of situations the average citizen might have little concern about, such as being at a party in which some of the attendees are smoking pot. This removal from aspects of the everyday helps ensure their protection against outside influences or pressure.

It is easy to take for granted just how crucial the role of an independent judiciary is to our country.

I was reminded of this on a trip my wife and I took to China some years ago. The trip included one week cruising the Yangtze River, from Shanghai through the Three Gorges Dam, up to our final destination, Xian, to see the famed Terra Cotta Soldiers. Each day, we would embark at different locations along the Yangtze to visit various points of interest. The night before each stop we heard from a Chinese university professor, who, in perfect English, gave wonderfully informative lectures on what we would be seeing the next day. The professor was a small man with heavy, horn-rimmed glasses hanging from a chain around his neck; his talks included important insights into China's history, literature, religion, culture, and the like.

After his lecture on the final night, I approached the professor to express my gratitude. In the ensuing conversation, I asked a question. Remarking on the great variety of subjects he had covered about life in China, past and present, I noted that he had never said anything about the rule of law. I asked him whether China had the rule of law. The professor looked at me quizzically and asked what that meant. I gave him a hypothetical. "Suppose you and I each own land that has a common border. I believe the property line should be drawn ten feet into your property, and you believe the line is correct where presently shown on maps. Is there a place we can go to have this dispute decided in a fair and impartial way?" He laughed and said, "No." I asked how such a dispute would be resolved in today's China. The professor leaned over and asked in a low voice, "Are you closer to the Communist Party, or am I?"

However, independence, while a mandatory prerequisite to the fair administration of justice, is not enough. However independent a trial judge may be, I am convinced that he or she cannot properly perform the role without first being a good person, whatever one's scholarly expertise, dedication, or judicial philosophy. It is a bona fide occupational qualification, however difficult it may be to define, quantify, or prescreen judicial candidates for. Whether this is equally true of appellate judges, who only deal with lawyers who appear before them occasionally and briefly in oral argument, I cannot say. I have neither sufficient experience arguing appeals nor actual relationships with appeals court judges to make that kind of assessment. But trial court judges, no matter how well-educated, dedicated, or driven, and no matter how objective they believe themselves to be, simply cannot do their job well if they cannot relate to the human condition.

Just as importantly, they cannot do their job well if they are not sufficiently aware of their own foibles and how they come across to, and impact upon, other human beings.

I will give examples of judges on opposite ends of this spectrum. Because what follows is based on one man's limited, personal, and admittedly subjective views, I confine my reporting to portraits of judges I am certain a substantial majority of my brothers and sisters in the New York City federal bar would readily recognize and very much agree with.

The most egregiously unqualified federal judge I have ever known of was the Southern District of New York's Irving Ben Cooper. His 1962 nomination to the court by President Kennedy was vigorously opposed by legal luminaries, such as former U.S. Attorney General Herbert Brownell. The New York Bar Association called him "temperamentally unfit." Who can know what political favor was being paid for his appointment, but appointed he was. Given his clear emotional instability, defense lawyers called him "Irving Ben Bellevue," after the New York City Hospital's notorious psychiatric ward.

I was fortunate enough to have never appeared before him, but Ken Kaplan had one matter before Judge Cooper he vividly recalls.

A week or so after an initial appearance before Judge Cooper in a credit card fraud case, Ken got a call from a Cooper law clerk. The clerk advised that the judge wanted to see the lawyers in his chambers. Ken asked when. The clerk said, "right now." Not quite sure what the emergency was, Ken dropped what he was doing and rushed to the courthouse, where he met the Assistant United States Attorney assigned to the matter. She, too, had no idea as to the purpose of the meeting.

The session began with the judge providing a long soliloquy about his career, including service on the Seaberry Commission (whatever that was). When he concluded, Judge Cooper asked Ken if he was aware of his reputation. Realizing that any answer would be problematic, Ken reluctantly said, "yes." Cooper then launched into a tirade "About your client." As Ken reconstructs it, Cooper went on to say, "He can go to trial if he wants, but remember, if he insists on a trial, a trial is like surgery. So we can wheel him into the courtroom on a gurney, but he can die on the operating table. Do you know what I mean?" After Ken said he understood, the stunned lawyers were abruptly excused.

Judges, of course, are not there to coerce guilty pleas. Quite the opposite. Under the Federal Rules of Criminal Procedure, a defendant does not have the right to plead guilty. It is only when the court is satisfied, after questioning the defendant under oath and in open court, that the plea is both knowing and voluntary, can a federal judge accept a defendant's guilty plea. The "Rule 11 Colloquy," as it is known, can sometimes take up to an hour or more, and that is how it should be. Judge Cooper's emergency session outbursts were surely threats one no other judge would have even thought of issuing.

Second only to Irving Ben Cooper in negative demeanor was the late Southern District of New York's David Edelstein. While defense lawyers were the primary recipients of his wrath, his nastiness could be both indiscriminate and difficult to understand. Early in my defense career, I endured a particularly contentious pre-trial hearing before Judge Edelstein. As my client and I left the courtroom, she turned to me and asked, "If Judge Edelstein is so unhappy in what he does for a living, why doesn't he just change careers?" That Judge Edelstein was aware of the impact he had on lawyers appearing before him is revealed in the following story.

Many years ago, I attended the New York Federal Bar Council's Thanksgiving Day Luncheon held at one of Manhattan's major hotels. Each year, the Federal Bar Council, a venerable professional group of civil and criminal lawyers active in the federal courts, hosts this event to raise money and awareness of its activities, usually by honoring some worthy lawyer or judge. I had been invited by Alvin Hellerstein, then a partner in Stroock, Stroock & Lavan, and later a Southern District of New York judge, to be his guest. Although I had long been a dues-paying member of the Federal Bar Council, I rarely attended its functions. However, I really liked and greatly respected Al Hellerstein (and still do), with whom I worked on various matters over the years before he became a judge. I accepted his generous offer.

One of the attractions for lawyers to shell out large sums of money to attend this and similar events is that usually seated at most of the tables is a federal judge, sometimes accompanied by his or her spouse.

Interacting with a judge on a social basis gives a lawyer the chance to make a positive personal impression on him or her, one that will hopefully translate into better treatment the next time they meet in the courtroom. While the degree to which any level of personal relationship can produce improved results will vary greatly, the fact that personal associations can really matter is yet another manifestation of the reality that "judges are human beings," who cannot help but be influenced to at least some degree, consciously or not, by their personal views.

At any rate, assigned to Alvin Hellerstein's table on this occasion was Judge Edelstein and his wife. I was seated to the left of Mrs. Edelstein, across from our host. At one point, Alvin, always gracious, told Mrs. Edelstein that I was a criminal defense attorney who regularly practiced in the Southern District. A little while later, as she and I spoke about this and that and nothing at all, she turned to me, and *sotto voce*, asked why it was that so many attorneys, particularly defense attorneys, disliked her husband so much. My initial thought was to ask how long she had been married to this man and how it was possible she did not know the answer to her own question. Instead, I replied, "That's odd, I have never heard that." Knowing full well my response was a good deal less than honest, our conversation abruptly ended and she focused her attention on the person seated to her right. The point of the story is that if Mrs. Edelstein needed to ask a complete stranger why her husband was so roundly disliked, he had obviously raised the very question with her, exposing a shocking lack of self-awareness. It made me feel sorry for both of them.

On the opposite end of the spectrum are federal judges who are simply paragons of the position, judges who lawyers are eager to appear before.

The elite of elite was the late Judge Edward Weinfeld of the Southern District of New York; he was a legal genius and real gentleman, revered by all. Indeed, Supreme Court Justice William Brennan was once quoted as saying about Weinfeld, "There is general agreement on bench and bar throughout the nation that there is no better judge on any court." How do you top that?

But judges do not have to be a Weinfeld to earn the respect and adulation of the bench and bar. One example for me was the late Eugene Nickerson in the Eastern District of New York. A descendant of President John Quincy Adams, Judge Nickerson, who looked every bit the patrician he was, enjoyed a notable career prior to taking the bench. He had been a progressive and highly successful

County Executive of Nassau County, New York (and thus possessed real social and political skills). He went on to a lucrative private practice with a major law firm then bearing his name, a law firm now known as Kramer Levin Naftalis & Frankel. I had numerous cases before Judge Nickerson as a defense lawyer, including one trial, and we had a good relationship.

In an appearance before Judge Nickerson at a pre-trial hearing defending a client in a tax matter, his personality and class came shining through. The prosecutor, for the first time, made a request of the judge that if granted, would do real damage to the defense posture at a potential trial. When the judge turned to me to reply, unfortunately I had nothing to justify him not giving the government what it wanted. However, I could not simply concede. Accordingly, I made, let's call it, a "creative" argument that at least gave some basis for a denial of the government's request. When I finished, Judge Nickerson smiled and looked down at me from the bench. He said, "Always on the cutting edge, aren't you, Bob." What he was saying in a humorous way, of course, was, nice try but you have got to be kidding. The point is, he ruled against me (and properly so), but did so while still being respectful and gracious.

Another especially gracious judge was Morris Lasker. An erudite, courteous, detail-oriented activist, Judge Lasker was known to the public at large for striking down the horribly squalid conditions in the New York City jails of the 1960s and sentencing the legendary financier, Ivan Boesky, for insider trading. For most lawyers practicing in the Southern District of New York, Morris Lasker was the judge you hoped would be assigned to your case.

While I never had the chance to try a case before Judge Lasker, one of my matters with him speaks volumes. I represented a printing company served with a grand jury subpoena for all of its records and files. In preparing the client's document production, I came across numerous letters and memos prepared by the company's in-house lawyer which I believed were covered by the attorney-client privilege, and thus shielded from production. As practice required, I set aside and generically identified these documents to the government in a "privilege log" and produced the log along with my production of the balance of demanded materials. As I expected, the Southern District prosecutors challenged this invocation and demanded the documents identified in the "privilege log" be produced to a judge to inspect *in camera* (Latin for a non-public proceeding, sometimes with only one party present), to validate or refute the protected nature of the withheld items.

Their challenge was assigned to Judge Lasker.

This was hardly my first (or last) time litigating attorney-client privilege and related issues, and I expected a call from one of Lasker's law clerks asking me to deliver the materials at issue to chambers, where they would go over the challenged items with the judge. I did, in fact, get a call from one of his clerks, but the request was to personally bring the original and one copy of the documents to chambers. I was asked to do so when I could devote enough time to be present for review.

When I arrived, I expected to sit with Lasker's clerk or clerks and briefly go over the items. Instead, Judge Lasker personally invited me into his chambers' conference area. Over coffee and tea, the judge, one of his clerks, and I went over each document, line by line, with the judge politely asking probing questions as to each, while his clerk took notes. When we concluded, he shook my hand, thanked me for my time, and said he would issue an opinion shortly. Two days later he upheld the invocation of privilege as to all documents but one.

The time Judge Lasker had taken personally, and his collegial yet detailed approach, just blew me away. Although the matter itself had no special significance, Morris Lasker wanted to make sure he fully understood my legal position as to the specific content of each document involved, so as to fairly adjudicate all issues raised, no matter how mundane, or how much of his time it required.

So, where does this leave our assessment of federal judges? Are they all well-suited for the position? Obviously, not. Are they "umpires" objectively calling balls and strikes? Hardly. Are they just "politicians in robes?" On the appellate level, that's a tough description to dismiss out of hand, especially in light of the politically charged way the two most recent Supreme Court Justices ascended to their positions. To fairly address the question, some perspective, however limited, is necessary.

The act of selecting federal judges is, and has always been, an essentially political one. As a general rule, the senators of the president's political party from the state in which a judicial vacancy occurs have historically played a significant role in selecting a nominee to recommend to the president. How this has played out has varied over time and under different political realities, such as whether both, one, or neither of the senators belong to the president's political party. A well-known example of how senatorial power was wielded in less tribal times was the so-called Moynihan Rule, named after the late New York Senator Daniel Patrick Moynihan. An exemplar of what a public servant should be, Moynihan is remembered for quotes such as, "People are entitled to their own opinions, but not their own facts," and "It is not ignorance that hurts so much as knowing all those things that ain't so."

Moynihan, ever the statesman, crafted a rule to assure evenhandedness in New York's judicial selections by granting the senator aligned with the president three out of four nominees, and the senator not of the same party one in four. During his four terms in the senate, New York always had one Republican (Jacob Javits and then Alphonse D'Amato) and one Democratic senator (Moynihan), with presidents of both parties. Thus, over time, the process benefitted both parties, while shafting neither. Although senators still play a major role in the selection of district court judges, their role in selecting circuit court judges has been meaningfully reduced over the decades, as both Republican and Democratic White Houses have taken control of that process to a substantial degree.

Finally, modern-era nominations for the Supreme Court have always been controlled by the president. While the political nature of the judicial selection process thus described has remained reasonably consistent over many years, it is only in more recent times that the pejorative "politicians in robes" description has become so pervasive.

Among a host of reasons, two stand out.

First, in the decades after World War II, presidents (especially, it seems, Republicans) have been unhappily surprised by the judicial positions ultimately taken by certain of their appointees to the High Court. According to legend, President Eisenhower believed his selection of Earl Warren as Chief Justice, who turned out to be an activist liberal, was one of the worst decisions he made as president. Similarly, Justice William Brennan surely proved to be far more liberal and activist than Eisenhower would have expected. Another striking example is President Ford's appointment of John Paul Stevens, a moderate, Republican, antitrust lawyer from Illinois, who led the liberal faction of the Supreme Court for decades. The last straw seems to have been Justice David Souter, appointed by the first President Bush. Souter, too, turned out to be far less conservative than anticipated, leading the frustrated Republican base to adopt the slogan, "No more Souters."

Since then, Supreme Court candidates and potential circuit court judges have been scrutinized and vetted by legal scholars and societies on the president's side of the ideological spectrum, and seem to require their blessing to qualify for potential selection. In the latest examples, both of President Trump's appointees to the High Court, Neil Gorsuch and Brett Kavanaugh, were drawn from the conservative Federalist Society's list of approved candidates.

The result is that from Justice Clarence Thomas on, Supreme Court Justices (and most circuit court judges) have, with limited exception, such as Chief Justice Roberts' decision on the Affordable Care Act, generally ruled in key matters as the president who selected them would have wanted.

The epitome of Supreme Court decisions underlying the "politicians in robes" label is, of course, the Rehnquist Court's 5-4 decision in <u>Bush v. Gore</u>, which decided the 2000 election for George W. Bush strictly along party lines. Making matters even worse, in rejecting the Florida Supreme Court's analysis supported by Al Gore and the Democrats, in order to obtain the desired result, the Republican-appointed majority turned its back on the great deference the Supreme Court had paid to state court rulings in decades of prior judicial opinions. As Justice John Paul Stevens noted in his famous dissent, "Although we may never know with complete certainty the identity of the winner of this year's Presidential election, the identity of the loser is perfectly clear. It is the Nation's confidence in the judge as an impartial guardian of the rule of law."

A second factor helping to create the view that our Supreme Court Justices are merely extensions of the politicians who chose them, is that in recent times politicians have adopted self-serving, cartoon versions of respected judicial analysis and theory to justify political goals. For example, a "strict constructionist" politician is almost certain to oppose abortion rights, gender equality, affirmative action, and other liberal positions.

Wrapping their policy beliefs in a high-sounding theory of constitutional construction gives politicians a veneer of scholarly objectivity to both cover and justify their purely political or personal views. Unfortunately, it also serves to blur the lines between the judicial and the other two branches of government, despoiling the judiciary with raw politics.

With a judicial selection process so highly politicized, with Supreme Court and circuit court judges ruling so consistently in support of the policy positions of the politicians who selected them, and with politicians using simplistic versions of legitimate theories of statutory construction to justify narrow, social, and policy preferences, the outcry against "politicians in robes" is hardly surprising. That this public outcry has a real basis in fact, that constitutional scholars like Linda Greenhouse now longingly look back to the court's past as "a time when not every decision was foreordained and ideology did not always reign supreme," is today's tragic reality.

However, to whatever extent the opprobrium pertains to Supreme Court Justices and circuit court judges, it has little applicability to their colleagues sitting in the U.S. District Courts. Indeed, it seems remarkable that, although they are selected by politicians, a meaningful majority of district court judges turn out to be as admirable and apolitical as they have proven over time to be. Perhaps it is a result of the narrower, more "nuts and bolts" nature of their role; their direct contact with the human beings impacted by their rulings; or it may be a consequence of a typical lack of prior judicial history available to skew the selection process.

Whatever the reasons, we are fortunate that these men and women, whatever their individual intellectual capabilities, backgrounds, personalities, belief systems and, yes, political affiliations, are able to perform as independently of our country's gaping political divide as they do.

Independence from political considerations, however, does not provide insularity from a given judge's history and personality. To the contrary, it can sometimes allow these individual factors to dominate the administration of justice in district court.

Chapter Twelve

LET 'EM WORK!

A trial judge's personality can meaningfully impact the conduct of a proceeding well beyond the specific rulings on evidentiary and legal matters emanating from his or her "judicial strike zone." I refer to the degree to which a judge, in the jargon of the courtroom, will "let you work." Some judges give wide latitude to lawyers, enabling their personalities and skills to shine through. Others hold counsel to much more rigid, limited presentations.

I long ago gave up trying to find a consistent, rational explaining the reasons underlying the stark differences in how judges conduct trials in their courtroom.

You would think that judges with experience trying cases before ascending to the bench would understand the challenges and give counsel wider berth, while judges with no prior courtroom experience would be less understanding and appreciative of the challenges involved. Yet some of the most restrictive judges I have encountered were former federal prosecutors, and some of the most generous had no prior trial experience. One would also think that a veteran judge would be more flexible than a more recent appointee, one less comfortable in the role and thus in greater need to maintain strict control. Again, many veteran judges I have tried cases before were extremely limiting, while certain neophytes quite the opposite.

The lack of a consistent explanation of what causes the divergence in no way impacts the reality, or mitigates its impact on the conduct and outcome of trials. Although, as in the trial before Judge Platt previously discussed, judicial intervention usually occurs during cross-examination, it can sometimes take place during summation, the most crucial part of the trial to which, as already noted, everything that occurred before was merely a prelude. As summing up was the climax of my courtroom performance, utilizing my greatest strength as a litigator, I found such judicial interruptions or limitations to be particularly unwelcome.

From early on, I learned the value of using my summation to connect with jurors on a personal level, enabling them to (hopefully) identify with me in some way. In this regard, one of my earliest role models was Jerry Lewis. No, not the legendary comedian. The Jerry Lewis I knew was a short man with a terrible, jet-black toupee that looked like an ill-fitting beret, a pencil mustache dyed the same harsh black color, and a Brooklyn accent as thick as I have ever heard. He was a paragon of "old school" courtroom lawyers. In today's world, even the most permissive of judges would not give him anywhere near the freedom he got "back in the day," and today's jurors would have a hard time relating. But Jerry was a fabulous character of his time, one who fearlessly used his distinct personality to dominate the courtroom.

As prosecutors, Ken Kaplan and I both tried cases against Jerry (Ken won, I lost) and became fans. We learned that Jerry had maybe a half-dozen set pieces for summation, and he selected among them depending on the jury's composition. For example, juries with a substantial number of African Americans heard his paean to Martin Luther King Jr. His cross-examinations had riffs as well. For a witness he was about to expose as a liar, Jerry, in full Brooklyn accent, would start off asking, "Are you a *truteful poyson?*" The answer would always be in the affirmative. He then would ask, "Do you believe in the Ten Commandments?" Again, the answer would be yes. "Do you believe in the commandment, 'thou shall not bear false witness against thy neighbor'?" The last affirmative answer would be followed by a brutal bashing that exposed lie after lie. In summation, he would loop back to the preliminary questions and tell the jury the witness had lied to their faces. While decades later this all seems corny at best, and he would never get away with his "shtick" today, Jerry was a unique entertainer and as successful as any of his peers.

When we were prosecutors, Ken and I would watch Jerry perform whenever he was on trial against one of our Eastern District colleagues and we could break away from our work. It was a great opportunity to be entertained and to learn. On one such occasion, Jerry was summing up in a trial before Judge Weinstein. He must have been in his early to mid-seventies. For at least a year, maybe two, Jerry had been telling jurors in summation that after however many decades in the courtroom, this was to be his very last trial. Ken and I went to Judge Weinstein's courtroom to see if he would do it again.

Sure enough, near the end of his summation, and with great emotion, Jerry declared that this was to be the last trial of his long career. Judge Weinstein broke in at that point and asked in a somewhat amused tone (and I paraphrase): "Mr. Lewis, are you telling the jury that because this is your last trial that they should acquit your client?" Lewis, without missing a beat (and these are pretty much his exact words) said, "Your Honor, I can think of no finer way to go out."

While I never had the showmanship or sheer gall of a Jerry Lewis, over the years I developed my own method for trying to reach jurors with set summation pieces, to varying degrees on a personal level, using personal anecdotes. I had maybe three or four of these pieces to choose from as appropriate. For example, when a government witness testified to things that seemed inherently inconsistent or contradictory, I cited my summers as a waiter at hotels in the Catskill Mountains in Upstate New York. Conflating a true story with an old joke, it went something like this.

> You know ladies and gentlemen, as I was lis-
> tening to Mr. _____ (a government witness) testify
> in this case, my mind flashed back to decades ago,
> and I was reminded of a man named Nathan Ross [a
> fictionalized, neutral name substituting for the real
> person]. I was 19 years old working that summer
> as a waiter at the Gilberts Hotel in South Fallsburg,
> New York. Mr. Ross and his wife sat at one of the
> tables I served during their one-week stay. Mr. Ross
> owned a delicatessen in Brooklyn and considered
> himself an expert on food. He had two complaints,
> which he registered loudly and often. First, the food
> I was serving him was terrible. Second, the portions
> were too small. Now, I wasn't the sharpest tool in
> the shed, but I kept asking myself, if the food was
> so bad, why could he not get enough of it? Now, I
> think you know why I thought of that man when I
> was listening to Mr. ____ (the government witness).

I would then go over the contradictions in the witness' claims and why, as a result, his or her testimony should be rejected. Beyond using the anecdote as a frame of reference to attack the credibility of the witness, I was trying to accomplish two things. First, get a laugh, and second, let the jury know that I wasn't always a high-priced lawyer in an expensive suit, and thus, someone to whom they might more readily relate.

By and large, I was fortunate to have judges give me a good amount of slack over the years. I sprinkled summations with personal anecdotes with regularity, and to what appeared to be great effect. One memorable exception was a trial before Judge Denise Cote, now a senior judge in the Southern District of New York. A really smart, incredibly hard-working, no-nonsense judge who I first met in the mid-1970s when she was a law clerk to Judge Weinstein, Judge Cote is in total control of her courtroom. No detail is too small to avoid oversight. Given her "judicial strike zone," defense counsel in criminal matters are rarely thrilled when she is assigned to their case. I had a number of matters with her over the years, but only one trial, emanating from what came to be known as the "Kennedy papers case."

I defended a man named Lawrence ("Lex") Cusack, accused in a highly publicized case of forging documents supposedly written by President Kennedy. Lex's father had been an advisor to the New York Catholic Archdiocese, and as such, had access to many private records of the Kennedy family stored there. Lex often accompanied his father on visits to the Archdiocese and, during certain of these trips, it is assumed that Lex had purloined certain original, personal Kennedy documents. The allegation was that from these authentic documents he forged numerous others, the most sensational of which dealt with a supposed secret trust set up by the president for Marilyn Monroe. Cusack sold these items for large sums of money until collectors began to believe they may have been forged. His undoing began in a televised interview with Peter Jennings, then one of the leading network anchormen on television.

I watched the "outtakes" of the interview in trial preparation.

Jennings skillfully put Cusack at ease in the warm-up that preceded the actual interview. Cusack surely must have felt this was going to be a friendly chat. When the warm-up ended, however, Jennings was loaded for bear. He produced a damaging piece of evidence casting serious doubt about the authenticity of a particular "Kennedy" letter. Lex was unable to meaningfully respond, and the interview went downhill from there.

Eventually, expert analyses of the ink, the paper, and the IBM typeface used, all shown to be unavailable until after JFK's death, established forgery. On top of that, handwriting analysis linked certain characteristics of Cusack's handwriting to the forgeries. If that was not damaging enough, the government had a witness who would testify that Cusack had admitted the fraud to him. While not quite the Guccione cartoon described earlier, it was as bleak a set of facts as I had ever encountered.

I met with the prosecutor, Paul Engelmeyer, now a Southern District of New York judge. We worked out a plea deal that capped Cusack's exposure to about half of the maximum term of imprisonment under the Federal Sentencing Guidelines, that is, the jail term I believed Judge Cote would impose if he were found guilty after trial. Yet, Cusack insisted on going to trial.

To my surprise, Paul Engelmeyer proved to be a skillful courtroom lawyer, in fact, among the most talented prosecutors I have ever faced. I say surprised because Paul is one of those lawyers with that 1 percent intellectual scholastic ability possessed by the appellate law clerks discussed earlier. In fact, Paul had clerked for both

Chief Judge Pat Wald of the D.C. Circuit Court of Appeals and for Supreme Court Justice Thurgood Marshall; this is a pedigree much more consistent with judges, law professors, and academics than highly talented trial lawyers. While not quite the same thing as being both a ballet dancer and a sumo wrestler, it is a rare combination. In any event, I did what I could to deflect the onslaught of brutal evidence skillfully presented.

The most positive reaction I received from jurors all trial came during summation, in my attempt to rebut Paul's focus on greed as the motivation for the fraud. He placed particular emphasis on Lex's lavish lifestyle, including a closet filled with Gucci loafers. The jury seemed to really enjoy my rejoinder. "I wonder; how many pairs of Gucci loafers does it take for somebody to be guilty? Three? Five? Seven? What if you just walk past the Gucci store? Are you guilty of conspiracy?"

Of greater ultimate significance, I had also prepared an anecdote, not one of my regulars, but one "Kennedy-oriented;" a story I planned to use to set up the conclusion to my remarks. I have long since forgotten the specific anecdote and the bridge it was intended to create, but it was based on my experience in my first year of law school as a student volunteer on Robert Kennedy's ill-fated campaign for president. I began with something like, "You know, ladies and gentlemen, I am probably the only person in this courtroom who actually worked for one of the Kennedys." That was as far as I got, as Judge Cote's stern voice called out, "No personal stories, Mr. Katzberg." I had never been cut off so abruptly in summation. I had no choice but to swallow my anger, plow ahead, and finish my closing argument in a more impromptu and less strategic way than I had planned.

Two days later, Cusack was convicted. One of the jurors told the press that it was all "too clear the documents were frauds."

Judge Cote ultimately calculated the Federal Sentencing Guidelines to increase his sentence some four months beyond the maximum I had feared.

The story ends some months later when I chatted with Judge Cote at a federal bar function. At one point in our conversation she asked me about the Kennedy reference I had made in the Cusack case. I explained that as a first-year law student in Washington, D.C., I worked afternoons in what was then called the Old Senate Office Building as a volunteer for Robert Kennedy's presidential campaign. My initial responsibility was to read the mail sent to him from people all over the country, and divide the letters into three categories: pro, con, and potentially dangerous. I was soon thereafter assigned to do research in the Library of Congress on subjects such as timber production in Oregon for the Oregon primary. Judge Cote then asked about the anecdote. I demurred, saying something like, "It is a better story for the courtroom."

Luckily, at that moment another attorney came over and the judge greeted her warmly. The matter was dropped and I excused myself. While she surely knew I was expressing my unhappiness at being limited in her courtroom, Judge Cote never took it out on me in subsequent matters I had before her.

CHAPTER THIRTEEN

WAR STORIES

"Back in the day," whenever seasoned criminal defense lawyers got together for any length of time, they would inevitably swap stories of their courtroom experiences. These men (and again, they were almost exclusively men in those days), were not only accomplished courtroom performers—they knew how to entertain outside of the courtroom as well. The ability to command the attention of respected colleagues helped to boost one's overall status in the group, and the telling of a really funny war story did just that. Beyond enjoying the spotlight, regaling colleagues with these stories was meant to do one of three things, sometimes all three: make a point, get a laugh, or make the narrator look good. Whether it was over lunch, waiting for a judge to take the bench, or schmoozing at some professional event, the stories they swapped helped cement status and relationships.

While many of these stories were inflated, conflated, or contained outright lies, they were so ingrained in the world these lawyers inhabited, and revealed so much about the lawyers themselves, that it is not possible to recreate that universe without including at least a sampling.

Here are three of my favorites, selected from the subset of stories that I know to be true.

The first was related to me independently by both Jimmy LaRossa and Gus Newman. Sometime in the late 1960s, Jimmy, Gus, and Jerry Lewis defended three bank robbers charged with a series of bank heists in Brooklyn. This was, of course, a really powerful trio. Another lawyer, a bumbling, inept, solo practitioner with a small office over a store in Queens, had been hired by a fourth defendant because that defendant could not afford better. The trial proceeded as anticipated, as the three pros did their thing and the bumbler, whose name I have long ago forgotten, did his. The jury came back and convicted all but the bumbler's client, who was acquitted of all counts. In a post-verdict interview, a juror told Jimmy and Gus that they had acquitted the fourth defendant because the jury believed that someone with a lawyer that bad just had to be innocent.

The second story comes from Ben Brafman. It relates to a case he tried in the early 1990s in the Southern District of New York. Ben was defending a notorious organized crime figure charged with committing a series of mob-related murders. In those days, a prominent feature of Ben's always-stylish wardrobe was shirts with collars connected by a prominent, gold pin. At trial the government called a parade of witnesses, each of whom testified to a murder or murders Ben's client was charged with. After the opening witness ran through the gruesome details of the first murder, the prosecutor asked the witness to look around the courtroom to see if he could identify the perpetrator, and if so, to please point him out. He motioned to the defense table and said, "He is the one sitting next to the man with the gold collar pin." The second government witness was asked the same question after his narration of another brutal mob murder, and he too, identified the perpetrator as "sitting next to the man with the gold collar pin." Just as the government's third witness was being sworn in to testify, the client leaned over to Ben and in urgent tones whispered, "Ditch the fucking collar pin, will ya!"

The final story comes from Ron Fischetti, and was told at a packed New York Council of Defense Lawyer's Memorial for Gus Newman. In the mid-1960s, Ron was a young lawyer just starting out. Gus, who by then was already one of the major defense attorneys in the New York State criminal courts, referred a client to Ron in a minor, simple matter. The client was to enter a guilty plea in Brooklyn Criminal Court to a low-level felony and be sentenced to probation. The fee, representing the biggest payday in Fischetti's young career, was a thousand dollars. Fischetti prepped the client for the plea the day before the court session, and reminded him to bring the fee to court the next day. The client showed up with a thousand dollars in cash. After the plea was taken and they parted company, Ron excitedly ran to the bank to deposit his first big fee. The bank teller refused to accept the deposit, telling Ron that the bills were counterfeit. Fischetti tracked the client down and confronted him, asking how it was possible for him to have a client so stupid as to pay his legal fee with counterfeit money. The client responded by asking Ron how it was possible for him to have a criminal defense lawyer so stupid as to want to deposit cash in the bank.

CHAPTER FOURTEEN

SHARP PRACTICES

In 1994, my second, and last, organized crime trial, United States v. Conte, provided an opportunity to use the Pat Tuite criminal defense lawyer riff. Conte was a three-defendant murder racketeering case before Judge I. Leo Glasser, a former Dean of Brooklyn Law School, and among the most thoughtful judges then sitting on the United States District Court in Brooklyn. Glasser is a short man with straight black hair, dark glasses, and a bow tie perpetually popping out from the top of his judicial robes. He looks every bit the legal (and Talmudic) scholar he is. Judge Glasser operates as a no-nonsense, by-the-book jurist, yet at the same time is always courteous and respectful to lawyers appearing in his courtroom. While I had a number of prior matters before him, this would be my first (and last) chance to actually try a case before Judge Glasser.

Jay Goldberg, now remembered by most people as Donald Trump's lawyer in the 1990s, had been hired to represent the lead defendant, Pasquale ("Patsy") Conte. Trump aside, Jay was an important courtroom figure, described in a 1991 survey of New York City lawyers and judges as "the best pure trial lawyer in town." He asked me to represent Patsy Conte's main co-defendant, Paul Graziano, and I quickly accepted.

The prosecution's case largely rested on its main witness, Sammy ("the Bull") Gravano, John Gotti's trusted number two, turned government informant ("rat"). Despite his brutal history, Gravano had proven to be a very successful witness for the government, one whose testimony had helped convict numerous Gambino crime family members, including John Gotti.

The chief prosecutor was John Gleeson, whose aggressive prosecution of the mob, and in particular, his successful prosecution of John Gotti, was by then well-known among the defense bar and beyond. Seeking to get some first-hand intelligence on my opponent, I contacted George Santangelo, a lawyer who had been up against Gleeson in the past. George and I had been co-counsel years before in a successful trial defense of a RICO prosecution in the federal court in Newark, New Jersey, before Judge Maryann Trump Barry. Although we never worked together again, I respected his talent, honesty, and judgment. What I heard from George about my upcoming opponent was not reassuring. I was on my guard.

At trial, John Gleeson proved to be a very smart, well-prepared, and very aggressive lawyer, who seemed comfortable in the courtroom. The essence of the government's case was establishing the three defendants' culpability for the brutal killing of a mob "associate" named Louis DiBono. Direct proof that any of the three defendants on trial had actually been involved in the DiBono murder did not exist, so the prosecution had to rely upon broad assertions by Gravano and other, more circumstantial, evidence. An important part of the latter was a series of secret tape recordings the FBI had made of John Gotti and his cohorts at the Ravenite Social Club in Lower Manhattan's Little Italy, the hangout then used by members of the Gambino family. Given the broad scope of federal criminal conspiracy law, the rules of evidence allow the government great latitude in what evidence can be presented, and the Ravenite tapes fit within that purview.

Significantly, among the Ravenite recordings Gleeson chose to play was an infamous rant of John Gotti against his lawyers, Bruce Cutler and Jerry Shargel. In his railings, Gotti called them unethical crooks and rats, and wanted to know why it was called the Gambino organized crime family, and not the Shargel or Cutler organized crime family. John Gotti's baseless rant about his lawyers had nothing whatsoever to do with any of the defendants on trial, the lawyers defending them, or the murder of Louis DiBono. It was, nonetheless, played to the jury as part of the government's case at our trial. It was within the rules to do so, but in the view of defense counsel, myself very much included, was a very low blow intended to tarnish the lawyers in the Conte case and prejudice us in the eyes of the jury.

In legal parlance, I believed Gleeson was guilty of "sharp practices," that is, conduct that while not unethical, was close to the line. It echoed what George Santangelo had warned me about. Of tactical importance, however, was that by playing the Gotti smear of lawyers, my opponent had unwittingly created an opening. I could now make the defense of my client, at least in part, a defense of the United States Constitution in general, and criminal defense attorneys in particular. Using Pat Tuite's lawyer's homage to defense lawyers from the Marvin Glass trial, I went after Gleeson's tactics in my summation. Scott Leemon, now an established criminal practitioner in New York, was then a law student working as a paralegal on Jay Goldberg's Patsy Conte defense team. He sets the stage.

"Judge Glasser set a strict schedule for summations. We started

9:30 in the morning and would run until at least 6:00 that evening. It was right around 5:00 when it was Katzberg's turn. We were all, including the jury, really starting to sag. They looked like they were done. Jay had just finished giving his summation, fighting through a serious head cold. The mood at the defense table was down."

I approached the podium used for summations having to surmount three immediate hurdles. First, I needed to get past my personal unhappiness that Judge Glasser insisted on proceeding so late in the day, depriving me of a good night's sleep and the chance to speak to a well-rested audience. Second, given the lateness of the hour, I had to pare down, on the fly, the least important parts of the summation to shorten the overall presentation. Finally, I needed to address the jury's obvious displeasure at having to endure yet another summation after a very long day, hint that it was a feeling we shared, and quickly move on. The trial transcript reflects those concerns and my approach.

Let me begin my summation, and I realize it's late in the day and you have heard a lot. It's at the end of the trial. You've been here since 9:30 this morning and you've been here for almost a month now, and I know you are tired. I know it's going to be difficult.

I'm not looking for your sympathy, only your indulgence, because this is a very important time for Paul Graziano and I would appreciate your bearing with me.

I want to begin my summation by going back to my opening remarks when I first had the opportunity to address you when the trial began. I think you will recall what I said in my opening, an opening statement is like a promise from a lawyer to the jury. It's almost like a contract between the lawyer and the jury where the lawyer says, ladies and gentlemen, the evidence in this case is going to turn out in a certain way. I predict the evidence will show something, or that it won't show something. And if my prediction proves accurate, my promise as to what the evidence is going to show proves correct, at the end of the case, I'm going to ask you to vote your verdict for my client. Well, I am here now to redeem the promise I made in my opening.

I hope to establish to your satisfaction during the course of this summation that the evidence has turned out precisely as I predicted it would. That my prediction as to what would happen, what would be shown and what would not be shown, has come true.

I'm sure that you recall that I predicted that the case against Mr. Graziano was Sammy Gravano alone. You will recall that I said in my opening that the case against Mr. Graziano begins and ends with Sammy Gravano.

You will hear all kinds of evidence, hear of surveillances, see videos, photographs, you will hear testimony from an expert witness, you will hear testimony from other witnesses, but I predicted none of that would involve, would claim to any extent at

all, that Paul Graziano was involved in the murder
of Louis DiBono, and I think that has come true.

You may also recall that I predicted that you
would hear a lot about who knows who. That you
would be seeing and hearing a lot about who goes
where, but that you would be seeing and hearing
very little about who did what. And I think that prediction has come true as well.

For the next 40 minutes or so, I took the jury through the spe-
cifics that supported these assertions, setting up what was to be the
most potent, yet delicate, issue to be addressed, the tactics chosen
by the prosecutors. It came near the end of my closing remarks. I
spoke of the numerous attempts the prosecution had made to gloss
over a lack of real evidence against the men on trial by trying to
inflame the jury using guilt by association. That is, that the defendants on trial were associated with notorious people like John Gotti
and Sammy Gravano, who were involved in, among other things,
organized crime-related murders. Again, quoting from the official
trial transcript, that part of my closing statement ended with,

They want you inflamed, they want you prejudiced and maybe you will overlook the fact that there
is no evidence of murder.

At that point I left the place where the lawyers stand for summations, a podium at the foot of the jury box, and walked to the nearby,
long, dark wood table where the members of the prosecution team
sat. I stood directly behind John Gleeson. Having discarded the podium, I stood over my clearly surprised opponents, federal prosecutors
and FBI agents alike, with no notes, and called their leader to task.

I do not recall whether I had planned to leave the podium for this part of my remarks, or if it was a spur-of-the-moment inspiration. My strong surmise is that it was the latter. It was a dramatic and extraordinary departure from accepted courtroom protocol that few judges would ever allow, especially given how personal it made things. Fortunately, Judge Glasser allowed me to do it. Raising my voice directly above Gleeson's head as I stood over him, I started to build the bridge to the Pat Tuite piece:

> Speaking of inflammatory, what in the world do we make of those lawyer tapes, the tapes about what Gotti said about his lawyers? Why did we hear all of that? What does what Gotti said about his lawyers have to do with who killed Louis DiBono? The lawyers are rats, they are crooks, they do unethical things, representing people who are supposed to be members of the Gambino crime family. Why did we hear that? Perhaps the same tactic of guilt by association the government is using against the defendants here, they are using against their lawyers too.

I could almost feel the anger rising from his head as Gleeson rose twice to object. The judge just ignored him. I like to think Judge Glasser was as into it as I was. So, I continued, launching into an extended version of Pat Tuite's paean to lawyers.

> I want to address that as quickly, as directly as I can and get it out of this case because it doesn't belong. Let me start by saying that I am proud to be a criminal defense lawyer. I'm proud to be a lawyer who defends people who are charged with crimes.

You know there are a lot of wonderful professions that people have in this country, doctors, nurses, teachers, professors, athletes, people in the arts, people who work in government, all wonderful, each and every one.

But you know there is only one profession, only one, that is guaranteed by the United States Constitution. And that is lawyers who represent people who are charged with crimes. So fundamental, so significant, how important that function is to everybody's liberty, yours, mine, Mr. Gleeson's, that the Sixth Amendment guaranteed that anyone accused of a crime will be represented by a lawyer.

The Constitution does not discriminate. It does not say only certain kinds of charges, or allegations require a lawyer. And the Constitution doesn't discriminate by talking only of certain kinds of people who can be represented by lawyers.

And so, from time to time, members of my profession, people who do what I do, are called upon to represent people who are alleged to be members of organized crime, who are alleged to have committed crimes in furtherance of organized crime. From time to time, lawyers who represent people charged with crimes represent doctors and teachers and businesspeople and accountants and firemen and secretaries and clerks and bus drivers who are charged with crimes.

From time to time, members of my profession are called upon to represent FBI agents who are charged with crimes. There was even a case six years ago in Manhattan when a member of my profession was called upon to represent an Assistant United States Attorney who was charged with a crime.

So, I'm proud of what I do, I'm proud of my profession and there is nothing that John Gotti said about his lawyers which changes that one iota. And there is nothing that John Gotti said about his lawyers that has anything to do with me or [the names of all of the other defense lawyers in the case], nothing whatsoever.

Again, the government can prove its case any way it wants, but the method it has selected, how it is going about its business, speaks volumes, volumes to how weak their case really is.

This is how Scott Leemon describes the impact. "I have never seen anything like it. Not only did Katzberg deliver his scathing rebuttal standing over Gleeson, he spoke without notes, adding a strong theatric element to it all. Jay kept waiting for Judge Glasser to intervene, but he just ignored Gleeson's objections. It was a dramatic change of momentum. We left the courtroom on an unexpected high."

The case ended in a hung jury, as a minority of the panel refused to convict. I like to think my summation, in particular the defense of the criminal defense role, played an important part in that.

Judge Glasser called it the best summation he had ever heard in all of his years on the bench. As the subsequent events described next might indicate, it is unlikely that John Gleeson felt the same way.

CHAPTER FIFTEEN

ROTHSTEIN

Only two of the cases I tried over the years were civil, as opposed to criminal. One was my defense of Patrick Murphy, a partner at Goldman Sachs who was a "specialist" on the New York Stock Exchange. A specialist represents a particular stock on the floor of the NYSE and takes orders, at his post, both in person from "floor brokers" and electronically from all over the world, to buy or sell that stock. Pat, along with another half dozen or so specialists, including former N.J. Governor Chris Christie's brother Todd, were alleged to have traded ahead of customer orders to their financial advantage and their customers' disadvantage, thus violating securities rules.

It was liberating not having to worry about my client going to jail if we lost. Plus, I enjoyed working with the especially strong group of lawyers representing the other specialists, including the impressive Paul Schechtman. That *The Wall Street Journal*, in reporting on the trial, described my defense of Pat Murphy as the "highlight" of the defense case, and most importantly, that the judge ultimately dismissed all claims lodged by the SEC against him, made the experience all the more rewarding.

The other civil case, one that I initiated, did not ultimately turn out so well.

Teddy Rothstein had been in the "adult entertainment" business long before the internet made such material as ubiquitous as it is today. He was a successful purveyor of "X-rated" magazines and videos throughout the country. Teddy got caught up in a sting operation in Tallahassee, Florida. He was charged by federal prosecutors there with conspiring to violate federal obscenity laws. The principal witness against him was an even more prominent adult entrepreneur from California, Mark Carriere, who cooperated with the government to mitigate his own exposure. Ultimately, Rothstein got the Florida charges dropped, but remained angry at what he was certain were lies Carriere told about him that were a substantial basis of the charges. I represented a co-defendant, Donald Sarnblad, in the Tallahassee prosecution. Sarnblad, a former associate of Rothstein, was unable to afford my legal fees. As a result, Rothstein paid my pre-trial fee. Ultimately, the charges against Sarnblad were also dismissed before trial.

Some months after the Tallahassee dismissals, Rothstein came to see me and asked if I would represent him in a wrongful prosecution lawsuit he wanted to bring against the government. Given the long odds involved in overcoming the substantial legal impediments to any such suit, I declined. He left my office disappointed, but I think he understood where I was coming from, and seemed to give up the idea.

In the days that followed I kept thinking about Rothstein's dilemma and how it fit into a broader context.

The advent of the Federal Sentencing Guidelines in 1987 introduced a greatly increased impetus for those under federal investigation or indictment to cooperate with the government. If you pleaded or were found guilty after trial, the Guidelines made imprisonment much more certain than before—and for meaningfully longer periods of time. Despite sharp declines in overall crime rates between 1990 and 2000, which was the first full decade after implementation of the Guidelines, the federal prison population of the United States doubled. Between 2000 and 2004 it nearly doubled again. The introduction of mandatory minimum sentences also played a significant role, as the Guidelines incorporated these severe measures into the new regime. All of this helped to create a frightening reality—by a wide margin, the United States has the highest incarceration rate in the world.

The only way out from under the Federal Sentencing Guidelines is contained in section 5K1.1. That section grants the government authority to move the sentencing court to "downwardly depart" from the otherwise applicable guideline sentencing range and give a defendant a more lenient sentence if the defendant cooperated with the government. Cooperation under the Guidelines means providing "substantial assistance" to the government. "Substantial assistance" in turn, means more than just fully admitting one's own guilt, although such an admission is a mandatory prerequisite. Cooperation means providing evidence against others. The more people you inculpate, or the more important the objects of your cooperation are, the more valuable your cooperation. The more valuable the cooperation, the more potentially lenient your ultimate sentence. The decision whether to make the motion to "downwardly depart" is at the sole and unbridled discretion of prosecutors.

As the full impact of the Guidelines came into focus in the late 1980s, the criminal defense bar, among other segments of the criminal justice system, became increasingly concerned with various aspects of the new regime. One substantial concern was the prospect that the incentive to cooperate might be an incentive to lie, or at least distort the truth. Ken Kaplan and I reviewed the Rothstein situation through that prism at some length, and initially agreed that there was nothing to be done given the level of immunity from liability that is necessarily, and quite appropriately, afforded to prosecutors.

As was typical of our relationship, I would often have ideas that were somewhat "out of the box," ideas that I would run by Ken. More often than not, he would point to an aspect of the situation that I had either given too little importance to or missed entirely. The Rothstein discussions must have triggered something in my brain, as it later occurred to me that we could avoid the obstacles inherent in suing the government for wrongful prosecution by suing Carriere individually, and thus leave the government out of it. Carriere was seemingly a wealthy man, so an eventual judgment against him would have real value.

There was no meaningful precedent for this kind of lawsuit. Ken, our associate Mayo Schreiber, Jr., and I reviewed the few potentially analogous precedents and legal authorities to determine the elements of the new offense we would ultimately have to prove in court. We eventually concluded that our novel approach was tenable. However, Ken and I were concerned that Rothstein, a "pornographer," would have little personal appeal to a jury. We feared that a jury considering its verdict (should we get that far), might well have "a plague on both your houses" attitude and either not grant Rothstein any award, or a meager one at that. It was for that reason we included a punitive damages claim to our filing. We hoped that if the case would go well enough, the jurors might feel a level of moral outrage and focus on punishing Carriere and not necessarily on rewarding Rothstein.

It was still a long shot, but Ken and I agreed that we should not pass up the chance to do something unique and something we both believed might ultimately provide a helpful balance to the criminal justice system. It would take up a chunk of my time without the kind of financially security we normally required, but in the end, we decided to go for it.

We filed our complaint in the federal district where our client resided, which was the United States District Court for Eastern District of New York. Once a civil complaint is filed, it is randomly (and now electronically) assigned to one of the judges of the court. Our case was assigned to Judge Nina Gershon. A graduate of Yale Law School, Judge Gershon was known as a low-key, detail-oriented, hard-working judge who was neither pro-government nor pro-defense. As an "umpire" she seemed to have a genuinely neutral strike zone. I had never tried a case before her, but I spoke to numerous colleagues who had. Of greatest importance to me, they uniformly reported that she gave lawyers reasonable latitude to try their cases. The common view was that we were fortunate to have her.

Judge Gershon presided over the trial that followed in a manner consistent with her reputation. The jury came back and awarded Rothstein $300,000 in compensatory damages and $1 million in punitive damages.

The verdict was trumpeted in the media.

On the front page of *The New York Law Journal* (the daily "Bible" for New York lawyers) the banner headline was, "Federal Informant Hit with $1.3 Million Verdict." In a *New York Times* article dated April 20, 2002, the headline read, "Jury Holds an Informer Responsible for his Lies." It quoted numerous legal luminaries as to the significance of the verdict. For example, Harvard Law School professor Charles J. Ogletree, Jr. was quoted as saying, "It really opens up a whole new avenue for protecting defendants' rights. This verdict sends a serious message." The message was what Ken Kaplan and I had hoped for, that the increasing pressure to cooperate in federal court must not be used as a license to lie.

The Rothstein verdict was also very much a personal triumph, and I greatly appreciated the accolades I received from my peers. Especially gratifying was an extremely generous letter I received from a colleague I had only heard about, renowned Los Angeles criminal defense lawyer Barry Tarlow. It hits home when one of the nation's most respected criminal defense lawyers writes to say that you "deserve to be applauded by the entire defense bar."

Exceedingly few lawyers ever create a new legal theory to vindicate individual rights. I not only joined that select group, but turned my new, theoretical construct into a seven-figure reality in the four corners of the courtroom.

From early on in the Rothstein matter, I consulted with Elkan Abramowitz, a partner at Morvillo, Abramowitz, Grand, Iason & Anello, P.C., a premier white collar and civil litigation boutique law firm in New York. For decades, Elkan was, and still is, one of New York's best-known litigators. He is a legal scholar with a regular column in the *New York Law Journal* on recent developments in the criminal law. I greatly valued his advice in this and other matters, because Elkan has the kind of 1 percent scholarly intellect, as previously observed, that I felt was missing from my own skill set. As I opined previously in these pages, I do not believe it possible to be a really good trial court judge without being a good person. However, it is surely possible to be a top-flight lawyer and a real s.o.b. at the same time. With Elkan Abramowitz, his extraordinary legal talents are matched only by his gentlemanly class. Because he believed in the overall significance of the Rothstein case, Elkan graciously agreed to handle Carriere's expected appeal at a steeply discounted, "professional courtesy" rate.

As it turned out, Carriere's formal appeal seemed to raise no issues of real concern. The only point with any potential merit had not been raised by Carriere's attorneys at trial before Judge Gershon. Thus, under basic principles of law, it had not been "preserved" for appellate review. While we were concerned that a pro-government panel of appellate judges would be loath to uphold new case law that potentially hindered prosecutors, we felt on solid ground with any reasonable break as to who would be hearing the appeal.

In the Second Circuit Court of Appeals, after the appealing party files a "notice of appeal," both sides get a scheduling order from the clerk's office dictating when the legal briefs must be submitted by each side. A subsequent order notifies the parties of the week they are expected to appear before the court to argue the case. The actual date of oral argument comes sometime thereafter. The typical case is heard by three of the Second Circuit judges; sometimes a district court judge will be part of the three-judge panel, sitting "by designation." This additional staffing allows the circuit to better handle its workload. It is also a "perk" for district judges to sit on the higher court.

The day of the oral argument, Elkan and I rode the courthouse elevator to the 17th floor where the majestic Second Circuit courtroom looms over lower Manhattan. After checking in, we entered the anteroom where the lawyers wait for the calendared cases to be called. It was there that the chalkboard announced the panel hearing appeals that day: John Walker, Chief Circuit Judge; Rosemary Pooler, Circuit Judge; and John Gleeson, District Judge; sitting by designation. That's right, the same John Gleeson who I stood over and castigated in open court some years before, had become a federal judge, and was now assigned (by what fate?) to sit by designation on the Rothstein appeal. I was sick.

It was a really bad draw.

Judge Walker, appointed to the Second Circuit by his first cousin, President George Herbert Walker Bush, had a well-deserved, strong, pro-prosecution reputation. Judge Pooler, appointed by President Clinton, was less problematic, but there was no way to predict how she would react to our novel lawsuit. It was Gleeson, however, who gave me the most concern.

I explained to Elkan what had transpired in the trial before Judge Glasser and my own negative feelings about Gleeson. Elkan took it all in, but reminded me that, since taking the bench, Gleeson seemed to have gone out of his way to get past his "tenacious, win-at-all-costs prosecutor" days. I agreed, but expressed my strong belief that beneath the surface, he was who he was, and that did not bode well.

Elkan seemed willing to give Gleeson the benefit of the doubt as we debated whether to make a motion to recuse him from the case. A "recusal" motion would ask that he step down from the case, given the potential of bias against me resulting from my criticism of him in the Conte trial. We agreed that any such motion would fail, as Gleeson would surely downplay what happencd, say he harbored no ill will, and that in any event, what happened in the past was too attenuated to meet the "actual or potential conflict" recusal standard.

Elkan then raised the prospect that Gleeson might, himself, step down under the "appearance of propriety" standard. This is when, even in the absence of actual prejudice, the mere appearance that there may be bias is sufficient for a judge to step down from a matter. I discounted this as overly optimistic, but Elkan wanted to give Gleeson the benefit of the doubt, and remained hopeful he might step aside. In any event, with the oral argument just minutes away, we had neither time nor anything practical to go on.

There was no real choice but to proceed as though there had been no history.

Elkan handled the oral argument at his usual high level, dispatching Carriere's appellate points with relative ease. The tenor of the questions Chief Judge Walker directed at Elkan, however, made me feel uneasy. At the outset, Gleeson nodded to me at counsel table. That was our only interaction. My name never came up during the oral argument, or in any of the questions from the court. That was hardly surprising, as my conduct was not an issue raised by Carriere during the trial or on appeal.

In the cab ride back to our respective offices, I continued to express my fear that the panel would find some way to overturn the result. I was certain that Walker was against us and that Gleeson would want to reverse the verdict on philosophical grounds even without the personal history. Elkan was more sanguine, yet concerned. As we parted company that day in early February 2003, the mood was somber.

Given the ultimate outcome, our feelings were more than justified.

In June 2004, I was in the midst of the Mark Belnick trial. It had been almost seventeen months since the Rothstein oral argument in the Second Circuit, and still there was no opinion. Seventeen months is far longer than it usually takes to hear from the circuit, especially given the straightforward nature of the issues presented on appeal, and the fact that there was ultimately no dissent to slow down the opinion drafting process.

We were in morning recess at the Belnick trial and the Rothstein appeal could not have been further from my mind. I walked over to the courtroom deputy's desk and asked to borrow his copy of the *New York Law Journal*.

There it was on the front page.

The Second Circuit, in an opinion written by Judge John Gleeson, reversed the Rothstein trial verdict, overruling Judge Gershon's findings of fact and conclusions of law to hold that we had not proven our case.

Most troubling, the opinion went out of its way to criticize me, by name, for conduct that in its most charitable form, can be called sharp practices. In the exceedingly low number of appellate opinions that criticize the conduct of attorneys I had seen over the years, the attorney's name is almost never mentioned. Usually the reference is to "trial counsel" or some other generic term. Here, my name was mentioned repeatedly (four times in just one paragraph). I was criticized for alleged conduct that was never raised by my opponent on appeal (or at trial), undoubtedly because it never occurred. While it is never a good time to face such an unusual and baseless public scolding, being on trial in a major case could not have been worse timing for me.

I used available weekends during the Mark Belnick trial and the days that followed his exoneration to scour the panel's opinion and the underlying record. The opinion totally mischaracterized my conduct in the pre-trial depositions. Even worse, it turned a blind eye to the contrary facts in the trial transcript that simply stared in the face of anyone actually reviewing that record. The Gleeson opinion states:

> Katzberg's conduct in the district court is even more troubling. Asserting that Rothstein had no part in Sarnblad's agreement, Katzberg argued that the only evidence to the contrary 'are two cover letters from Sarnblad's attorney, each rank hearsay . . .' Had

Katzberg been more forthright that 'Sarnblad's attorney' had been *Katzberg himself,* and that his fee had
been paid by Rothstein, the district court might have
better understood that Rothstein and Sarnblad had
made a package deal with the prosecutor.

The letters in question, both trial exhibits, were on my law
firm's letterhead and signed by me as Sarnblad's lawyer. As such,
Judge Gershon knew from the face of the letters what the court of
appeals stated I hid from her. Indeed, my authorship of these letters
had been openly discussed between trial counsel and Judge Gershon
in open court, and was there in the trial transcript for all to see.

Even more directly, the assertion that I concealed from Judge
Gershon my role as Sarnblad's attorney in the Tallahassee matter,
and the fact that Rothstein paid my pre-trial fee, is directly contra-
dicted by the trial transcript. The transcript is, of course, the key
document in any appellate review. The following are questions I
asked and the answers Sarnblad gave at the Rothstein trial on April
9, 2002, as shown in the official transcript at pages 283-84.

Q. Now, did you hire a lawyer to represent you against those
charges contained in Exhibit 11 [the Tallahassee indictment]?

A. Yes I did.

Q. And who was that?

A. The lawyer at the time was you.

Q. Mr. Sarnblad, were you financially able to pay my fee?

A. No, I was not.

Q. And what did you do?

A. I went to Mr. Rothstein and asked to borrow the money.

Q. And how much money did you borrow?

A. Approximately $75,000.00.

Q. Was it a gift or a loan?

A. A loan.

Q. How much money have you paid back so far?

A. Nothing.

Q. So as of today, how much do you owe him?

A. $75,000.00

How the panel could have overlooked this key part of the trial record, or having read it, believed it consistent with the conclusion that I hid these very facts from Judge Gershon, is beyond comprehension.

We petitioned the court to reconsider.

In the meantime, I wrote personal letters to the trial judges in the Eastern and Southern Districts of New York whose opinion of me I felt was most important to preserve. In these letters I rebutted the criticism point by point. The judges' responses, both by phone and handwritten notes, were really gratifying. Particularly meaningful to me was the warm and generous note I received from Judge Glasser, who so to speak, was there at the creation. It made his support all the more significant to me.

I had an interesting follow-up lunch with another of the judges I contacted. I asked how it was possible for the entire panel, Gleeson notwithstanding, to have generated such a baseless and unfair opinion despite the underlying, contrary facts that literally stared them in the face. Although no stranger to the Second Circuit, having sat by designation himself, he had no satisfying answer.

He speculated that the panel quickly decided to reverse the

result and that Gleeson had either volunteered or was assigned by Judge Walker to write the actual opinion. Speculating further, and focusing on the unusually long delay between oral argument and the eventual opinion, the judge guessed that whatever draft opinions were submitted, the final version was held back by Gleeson for a long time. By the time June of 2004 rolled around, it had become a "back-burner" matter for the other two judges, and thus eluded real scrutiny. It was a reach, and we both knew it.

I asked whether he thought Gleeson had revealed to the other members of the panel his prior, negative interaction with me in the Conte case. The judge, while uncertain, strongly doubted it. He believed that if Gleeson had done so, it would have been very unlikely he would have been tasked to write the actual opinion, as neither of the other two had the potentially disabling "appearance of impropriety" burden.

As we were waiting for a response to our motion to the panel to reconsider its opinion, a completely amazing and totally unexpected thing happened. In an extraordinary step, Judge Gershon wrote the appellate judges "to advise the panel of what I believe is an injustice done to a member of the bar, an injustice which, I believe, could be corrected without any impact on the decision of the court."

Trial court judges simply do not write to the appellate judges who have reviewed one of their trials, let alone accuse them of committing "an injustice." Her astounding and courageous stand on my behalf came, needless to say, without a request by me. I was floored when I received the courtesy copy mailed to me and Carriere's counsel.

Elkan Abramowitz, whose knowledge of the Second Circuit over the last half century is about as extensive as any lawyer I know, describes Judge Gershon's letter to the circuit panel this way: "It never happened before and I would not expect it to ever happen again." To me, the letter was even more exceptional considering the fact that one of the judges she was taking to task (however diplomatically) was John Gleeson, a colleague of hers on the Eastern District bench, someone she would necessarily be seeing and interacting with on a regular basis for many years to come.

Her letter to the panel went on:

> I speak of footnote 5 of the opinion, which criticizes Robert F. Katzberg., Esq., counsel for plaintiff Rothstein, for having misled the district court as to his representation of Mr. Sarnblad in the underlying criminal case. **I assure the panel that I was not in the slightest way misled by Mr. Katzberg, nor did Mr. Katzberg make any effort to mislead me. On the contrary, although the Circuit obviously took a different view of the facts than I did, I was fully advised by the parties, including Mr. Katzberg, of the facts upon which the Circuit now relies. Moreover, throughout the pre-trial and trial proceedings, Mr. Katzberg proceeded in a thoroughly professional and ethical manner. Indeed, I do not recall any complaint from his adversary to the contrary.**
>
> In light of these facts, I thought it incumbent upon me to notify the panel, and urge that there be a correction which would eliminate the criticism of counsel's ethics. (Emphasis added).

Given this extraordinary, direct, and dispositive evidence that the negative conclusions drawn in a public filing about the conduct and character of a member of the bar were erroneous, one would expect that the panel would act quickly to remedy the injustice.

After all, the person who they asserted was fooled made it clear that she had not been, that there had been no attempt to deceive her, and that she had been made aware of the very facts at issue by the person accused of keeping these facts from her.

The expected remediation to clear the name of someone who at all times "proceeded in a thoroughly professional and ethical manner" never came. Instead, in an apparent sop to Judge Gershon, the panel slightly modified some of the language in its criticism of me. The baseless reproach, castigating me for a wrong I never committed, the panel's focus on a legal issue barred from appellate review by well-settled law, and the ultimate rejection of Judge Gershon's factual and legal findings, all remained.

Despite the unsettling, head-scratching nature of these events, there can no doubt that they occurred, and precisely as reported in this book.

My summation in the Conte case excoriating John Gleeson, just as I have quoted it, is preserved in the official Eastern District of New York transcript of that trial; the erroneous allegations made in the Gleeson Rothstein opinion are set forth in both press reports and the Second Circuit Court of Appeals's official archive of its filed opinions; Donald Sarnblad's testimony quoted from the Rothstein trial that directly refutes the Gleeson allegations is preserved, word for word, in the official Eastern District of New York transcript of that litigation; Judge Gershon's remarkable rebuttal letter to the court of appeals, a copy of which has been made part of this book, is an official filing in the Rothstein Second Circuit appeal.

Thus, we know with certainty what happened. What remains a mystery is the underlying dynamic that allowed it to happen.

Cross-examining a witness in <u>Rothstein v. Carriere</u>,
April 2002.

UNITED STATES DISTRICT COURT
EASTERN DISTRICT OF NEW YORK
UNITED STATES COURTHOUSE
225 CADMAN PLAZA EAST
BROOKLYN, NEW YORK 11201

Nina Gershon
United States District Judge

July 22, 2004

Roseann B. MacKechnie
Clerk of Court
United States Court of Appeals
    for the Second Circuit
40 Centre Street
New York, NY 10007

Re: Rothstein v. Carriere, Dkt. No. 02-7731

Dear Ms. MacKechnie:

I request that you send copies of this letter to the members of the panel in the above-captioned appeal, Chief Judge Walker, Circuit Judge Pooler, and District Judge Gleeson. I am taking the unusual step of writing to the members of the panel, not to express any thoughts about the reversal of the judgment, but solely to advise the panel of what I believe is an injustice done to a member of the bar, an injustice which, I believe, could be corrected without any impact on the decision of the court.

I speak of footnote 5 of the opinion, which criticizes Robert F. Katzberg, Esq., counsel for plaintiff Rothstein, for having misled the district court as to his representation of Mr. Sarnblad in the underlying criminal case. I assure the panel that I was not in the slightest way misled by Mr. Katzberg, nor did Mr. Katzberg make any effort to mislead me. On the contrary, although the Circuit obviously took a different view of the facts than I did, I was fully advised by the parties, including Mr. Katzberg, of the facts upon which the Circuit now relies. Moreover, throughout the pretrial and trial proceedings, Mr. Katzberg proceeded in a thoroughly professional and ethical manner. Indeed, I do not recall any complaint from his adversary to the contrary.

In light of these facts, I thought it incumbent upon me to notify the panel, and to urge that there be a correction which would eliminate the criticism of counsel's ethics.

Yours truly,

Nina Gershon

cc: Robert F. Katzberg, Esq.
    Randy Friedberg, Esq.

Letter of the Hon. Nina Gershon to the Clerk of the Court for the
Second Circuit Court of Appeals, July 22, 2004, regarding its opinion in
Rothstein v. Carriere.

Chapter Sixteen

THE KRIN

Having recounted the intense, "all or nothing," yet essentially theatrical experience that was life in the courtroom "back in the day," I have hopefully provided a meaningful understanding of the world we are slowly but surely losing. I would now like to examine how this new reality of disappearing trials has come to be, and what can be done about it. Before doing so, however, it would be helpful to broaden the perspective.

This book's discussion of the vanishing trial has been confined to federal court, and the steadily decreasing number of criminal trials over the past several decades in United States District Courts. There are three reasons for the focus on federal courts. First, federal district court is where a substantial majority of the nation's most complex and significant prosecutions are brought. Second, there does not seem to be a comparable decline in the criminal trials conducted in most state courts. For example, New York City's 2016 Annual Report of its Criminal Courts reveals little fluctuation in the number of criminal court trials between 2009 (169) and 2016 (185), with a low of 140 and a high of 209 in the years in between.

Third, with the exception of a few white collar state court trials like the Belnick and Singer cases previously discussed, my experience is almost exclusively in the federal realm. Thus, the greatest relevance of my courtroom experience to the problem at hand is necessarily federal-centric.

That the problem appears to be largely confined to our federal courts in no way diminishes its significance or the need for real concern. The medical equivalent of such thinking would be having no anxiety about a pancreatic cancer diagnosis because your lungs are clear. It is in district court where the legal muscle of the federal government is flexed, where the weight of the national sovereign is brought to bear most directly and powerfully on individuals, businesses, religious organizations, schools, and per the Constitution's Supremacy Clause, on state and local governments as well. For example, that the prosecutions of more than 30 individuals and entities charged with interfering with the 2016 presidential election were all brought in federal court is anything but surprising. Instead, it is a reflection of the power, recourses, reach, and mandate of the federal government.

However, it would be helpful to a full discussion of the scarcity of trials in federal court to include at least a slice of relevant state court reality. Comparing these parallel worlds will help to better identify the underlying causes of the federal problem. A full and complete discussion of the differences, interrelatedness, and overlap between state and federal criminal laws and practice would fill volumes, and such a discussion is both beyond my skill set and unnecessary to our purposes. A brief, generalized, overview will suffice.

There are two basic levels of criminal justice in the United States: federal and state.

On the federal level, everyone in every state and U.S. territory is subject to the mandates of the United States Code, including the criminal statutes contained in Titles 18 and 26. On the local level, each state has its own laws and regulations governing its inhabitants' conduct, including criminal prohibitions. Those convicted of federal crimes serve jail time in the federal prison system, while those convicted in state courts are incarcerated in state penal institutions. There are numerous examples, such as bank robbery and drug offenses, in which the same conduct can violate both state and federal criminal law.

Generally speaking, however, federal prosecutions, particularly in our larger cities, place at least an equal emphasis on white collar crimes such as tax evasion, money laundering, and financial fraud, as they do on narcotics offenses and the like. Only the more significant street crimes are prosecuted in federal court. In contrast, most state prosecutions deal with more every day, lower-level, street crimes.

Finally, and most importantly, because federal prosecutors have much deeper resources in terms of money, manpower, and expertise, they investigate and prosecute a very high percentage of the nation's most difficult, complex, and significant cases, whether they be white collar, organized crime, terrorism, firearms, or narcotics.

To compare the two systems, and better understand why a parallel, drastic decrease in state criminal trials seems not to have occurred, we can look to the experiences of a talented, veteran Brooklyn, New York-based criminal defense lawyer, Barry Krinsky, known to his friends and admirers as, "the Krin." Again, while the experiences of one lawyer, however extensive, can hardly reflect the totality of his professional world, they can help to provide useful insight into that world.

Barry has been a friend of mine since our Brooklyn College days. The Krin began his legal career in 1969, representing indigent defendants as a lawyer for the New York State Legal Aid Society.

In 1971, he began representing a similar clientele in federal court, in the Eastern District of New York, as an attorney for the Federal Defenders Service. Once he left Federal Defenders for private practice, however, his work became overwhelmingly state-based. This is so even though as an experienced defense attorney in federal court for nearly four years, he is one of a small subset of state court practitioners completely comfortable in federal court. Over the decades, his practice has been largely comprised of murder, gun, and narcotics cases. The federal portion of his work has been exclusively confined to defending his clients against federal analogs of his state court cases generated by the Eastern and Southern Districts of New York.

Krinsky, like almost all state court lawyers defending street crimes, has a different business model than white collar, primarily federal court, practitioners. He has no need for a large, fancy office in Manhattan, the expense of associate attorneys, substantial staff support, high-end computer systems, employee health programs, profit sharing plans, and the like. At Kaplan & Katzberg, we had just that kind of operation, with spacious, well-appointed offices high over midtown Manhattan, and all that went with it. It is what our high-end clientele expected and our practice required. Our monthly overhead was well in excess of $50,000; that is, we needed to take in that much every month before the partners took out a dime. Barry Krinsky's one-person office in downtown Brooklyn comes with an overhead nowhere near that. Just as importantly, he does not have to spend the precious time necessary to run a larger operation.

Lastly, the business model for practitioners like the Krin is a volume practice, that is, a practice primarily made up of a large number of lower to modest-fee cases. In contrast, Ken Kaplan and I ran a low-volume, high-fee practice, substantially comprised of more complex, data-intense matters, as is typical of federal, white collar lawyers.

As a result of these factors, the Krin has had far more opportunities to try cases than I did. He estimates that he has tried more
than 400 criminal cases over his career, an astronomical total.

Let's break down his numbers. Before 1990, of the total caseload he carried, perhaps 25 percent were federal and 75 percent
were state. Of those cases, he estimates that about 10 percent of
his federal cases went to trial, while some 25 percent of his state
cases were tried. Since 1990 (the first full decade of the federal court
trial decline), Krinsky estimates he has tried perhaps 5 percent of
his federal cases, while approximately 20 to 25 percent of state cases have gone to trial. Thus, the percentage of his federal trials has
been cut in half, while the state percentage has dropped only a bit.

In telephone and email interviews, I tried to explore with him
the underlying reasons for the dichotomy.

> **Q.** Why do such a high percentage of your trials take place in
> state criminal courts?

> **A.** Because in the state system, you can win. Over the many
> years, I won a lot more of these trials than I lost.

> **Q.** How is that?

> **A.** There are many reasons. In the state system, you interact
> with the jury in *voir dire*, and get to shape its members and
> at the same time, plant the seeds of your defense as you
> engage them in the selection process. That is not possible
> in federal court where the lawyers are not involved. It is
> all done by the court and the process takes no time at all.

> **Q.** So it's the jury selection that makes the difference?

> **A.** There is much more than that, but it plays a role.

Q. What else?

A. Your client really gets slammed when you lose a trial in federal court.

Q. Anything more?

A. The Assistant District Attorneys are usually not as good as federal prosecutors, usually not as well-prepared, and for the most part, do not communicate effectively with jurors. The main witnesses for the state in my cases are almost always police officers, who are typically not well-prepared and not very good, and who usually have a past filled with enough official misconduct that I can really discredit them. It is a very different world than having to deal with FBI Agents and Assistant United States Attorneys in federal district court.

Q. Over the decades you have spent in the courtroom, have you noticed any material drop in the number of state criminal trials in your practice and overall?

A. Only a relatively small decrease.

Q. Why do you think that is?

A. Nothing in the state court has really changed all that much over the years.

Q. But today, don't you have to deal with things like science and technology that played a smaller role in the past? Don't the new technologies make defense work much more difficult, and therefore, make the risks of trying a case that much greater?

A. Yes and no. DNA has certainly impacted identification evidence, but we have always had fingerprints. It is rare to see emails, texts, and other electronic evidence in my kind of state court case, so the impact is greater in federal court, especially in white collar cases.

Finally, the Krin reports that he has not tried a single case in federal court in more than five years. His most recent federal cases had all been resolved by guilty pleas.

We seem to be left, then, with contrasting realities.

First, experienced trial lawyers representing defendants charged in state court seem to have been minimally affected, if at all, by the vanishing trial. At the same time, their federal court counterparts, most glaringly in white collar cases, have been substantially sidelined.

Second, jurors still play a key role in the state and local criminal justice systems, serving as the voice of the people to check prosecutorial overreach, primarily in the prosecution of street crime. However, they are now dangerously absent from the nation's most important venue for criminal justice, the U. S. District Courts, where the nation's most significant, complex, and precedent setting matters are decided.

Thus, it is in this most important of venues where citizens are losing their ability to meaningfully impact the exercise of governmental authority.

This loss of power has taken place without even a modicum of public concern. This is not a reflection of a desire among the populous to forsake its role in the top level of our criminal justice system; it merely reflects a lack of awareness.

CHAPTER SEVENTEEN
THE VANISHING TRIAL

How did it come to be that, unlike in state courts, trials have been disappearing from federal court dockets? If it is correct that, essentially, "nothing has really changed" in most state criminal justice systems, then a major change has occurred in the federal. That change was the adoption of the Federal Sentencing Guidelines in 1987.

It has been widely recognized by legal observers of all stripes that the main cause of the steep reduction of criminal trials in federal district court is the impact of the Federal Sentencing Guidelines. Indeed, legal observers identified this watershed as the main culprit in the alarming reduction of jury trials fairly early on. Some analyses have even described the Guidelines as the *sole* culprit. As explained a bit later, in my view this overstates reality. However, it is no coincidence that federal criminal trials began to disappear in the late 1980s with the advent of the Guidelines.

Broadly speaking, the Federal Sentencing Guidelines sought to achieve greater nationwide uniformity in sentencing persons convicted of federal crimes by creating a mandatory sentencing regime. That regime, overseen by the United States Sentencing Commission (devastatingly derided by Justice Scalia as a "junior varsity congress"), ascribes numerical equivalents to all federal offenses. Points are then added to that "base level" to account for individual characteristics of the particular offense. For example, if the offense involved "more than minimal planning," points are added to the total. Financial crimes incorporate into the calculation the amount of the "loss." This can add significant points to the total, as though somehow a bank robber who was lucky enough to find a million dollars in the bank's vault was committing a more serious crime than the less fortunate robber who arrived after the Brinks truck came and left, and found only a few thousand. Once the "total offense level" is calculated, the ultimate sentencing range (in months) is governed by the defendant's "criminal history," that is, the longer that history, the longer the mandated sentence.

Judges were required to sentence the defendant within the prison range corresponding to the total level thus calculated.

Of greatest significance, and consistent with the era's "law and order" political climate, these mandatory sentencing levels were usually much higher than sentences imposed before the Guidelines. Compounding the problem, before the Guidelines, incarcerated defendants generally served a required minimum of one-third of their sentence. The Guidelines regime requires 85 percent of the sentence imposed to be served. Thus, defendants now must serve more than twice the minimum of meaningfully higher sentences, resulting in significantly longer prison terms. The result has been staggering. For example, between 1988 and 2012, the length of sentences served by federal prisoners more than doubled.

Not surprisingly, this regime has been widely criticized. For example, in a 2012 speech given to the New York City Bar Association, previously quoted Southern District of New York Judge Jed Rakoff questioned the wisdom of using simple arithmetic to answer complex questions of punishment. He decried the resulting huge increase in incarceration rates, particularly for white collar offenses. "Has the nature of white collar crime . . . changed so much since 1987 [when the Guidelines came into effect] that the guidelines should be 500 percent higher? No."

An important factor in the explosive increase in our federal prison population is the Federal Sentencing Guidelines's incorporation of mandatory minimum sentences in numerous offense categories. These minimums remove any discretion from the sentencing court to impose a sentence below the mandatory number of years in prison, regardless of any mitigating factors that may otherwise exist.

The results of mandatory minimum sentences can be mind-boggling. Take, for example, a criminal defendant suffering from a serious, prolonged illness such as an advanced form of cancer. If convicted of a crime with a mandatory minimum sentence of, say, ten years, a judge has no choice but to sentence that defendant to at least ten years in prison. The Bureau of Prisons will assign him to one its few facilities offering some level of advanced medical treatment, where he will likely receive worse treatment than he would in the outside world, all while the U.S. taxpayer will be spending hundreds of thousands of dollars in just the initial years of incarceration trying to keep him alive eight and one-half years to complete his sentence.

Offenses covered by mandatory minimums include drug offenses, crimes committed by defendants with long criminal histories, and child pornography.

Congress has more recently taken small steps to reduce the impact of these penalties, such as the modifications contained in the Fair Sentencing Act of 2010, but the overall effect has been minimal.

In fiscal year 2016, the average period of incarceration for offenders who were convicted of an offense carrying a mandatory minimum penalty was 110 months in jail. This is nearly four times the average sentence (28 months) for an offender convicted of an offense not carrying a mandatory minimum sentence.

The additional burden of mandatory minimums on the overall incarceration rate is clear. In the four years between 1988, when the Sentencing Guidelines were in its second year, and 2012, the average time served by a federal inmate more than doubled, rising from 17.9 months to 37.5 months. Adding insult to injury, the cost to taxpayers ballooned to some $2.7 billion a year.

The overall damage is even greater still. Since the Guidelines put more people in jail for substantially longer periods, they have meaningfully impacted day-to-day operations of the federal criminal justice system. Pleading guilty and avoiding a trial reduces the Guidelines sentence by two levels (and in more limited circumstances, three), thus reducing the calculated prison range. Cooperating with the government, as discussed earlier, is the only potential way out of the strict regime, as it permits a judge, upon a motion from the government pursuant to section 5K1.1 of the Guidelines, to "depart downward" from the otherwise applicable range to the degree the judge deems appropriate.

That the Guidelines, after years of litigation, have become "advisory," not mandatory, has surely helped, although mandatory minimum sentences remain unaffected. Small "tweaks" by the Sentencing Commission to certain of the Guidelines' other objectionable aspects have helped as well. However, the regime that many believe sacrifices too much on the altar of uniformity (a goal not actually achieved) endures, as does the resulting steep decline in those defendants and defense attorneys willing to risk going to trial. Given a federal prosecutor's ability to resolve a matter with a reduced charge, one with substantially lower guidelines than the most serious potential charge, it is hardly surprising that so many defendants (and their attorneys) have become so trial-averse.

Immediately after the Guidelines were enacted and the benefits of cooperation started to become clear, a few defense bar colleagues refused to cooperate their clients as a matter of "principle." Such voices are rarely, if ever, heard today. Even the most "principled," aggressive, and battle-ready criminal defense attorney must ultimately do what is best for the client, not what serves his or her legal theology, ego, skill set, or pocketbook. As already noted, the lawyer's greatest gift to the client is judgment. Metaphorically speaking, deciding whether the client's best escape is to walk, take a bus, ride a bike, or catch a plane, is where the lawyer earns the fee. Since the Guidelines, escape from the worst consequences of a federal prosecution has often meant cooperation.

A case in point. I was referred a client who had just been indicted in a securities fraud case involving a hedge fund she was working for that ran a Madoff-like Ponzi scheme. Much like Madoff, the two principals misappropriated money invested in their fund for their own substantial enrichment, replacing those funds with newly invested money and doctoring the books accordingly. When market conditions after the 2008 stock market crash forced most of their clients to seek the return of their capital, hundreds of millions of their investment dollars were missing.

My client had been the fund's compliance officer, that is, the person directly responsible for ensuring that the fund's operations were fully compliant with all SEC and related regulations. While deceived to a substantial extent by the two principals, she knew enough of what was going on to be implicated. Her biggest mistake was to believe her bosses' promises to straighten things out over time. That, of course, never happened. Some days before I was retained, the FBI came to the fund's offices and seized all of the records. They interviewed her and, against her interests, she answered their questions. Shortly thereafter, all three were arrested and charged.

It did not take long in our initial interview to see the depths of the problem. The seized records and her own statements made both the underlying crime and her involvement all too easy to prove. Especially given the sensational nature of what had taken place and the unfortunate echo of the Madoff scandal, it would not be a good case to try. On top of it all, given her "gatekeeping" compliance role in the fund, the generous bonuses she got and the huge amount of money lost by investors, the Guidelines calculation would be very high. The result would be a scary sentencing range.

I brought up the issue of cooperation, telling her that in my view, one or both of her bosses might already be doing so, or at least thinking about it. She was a forthright person who made a good impression. I believed prosecutors would see her that way, especially after I prepared her for the grilling they would put her through. While I have represented clients over the years whose lack of honesty and inability to confront reality eliminated any prospect of cooperating, this client was quite the opposite. Moreover, there were other aspects of the matter that need not be reported here that I was confident would make her sympathetic to prosecutors and, ultimately, to most judges considering her punishment.

Time was of the essence. If one of the other two had already made a deal to cooperate we might be out of luck. She gave her approval and I called the prosecutor, Southern District of New York AUSA, John O'Donnell. We arranged to meet that afternoon. John was a real pro, and we made a deal to cooperate.

Ultimately, both hedge fund partners pled guilty. One received an initial prison term of 20 years, the other 10. Our case was assigned to a judge with the kind of "judicial strike zone" and temperament I had hoped for. Based on her cooperation, in lieu of a prison term, the judge sentenced my client to one year of unsupervised probation.

A year or so later, I learned that the lawyer for the fund partner who had received a 10-year sentence had an appointment to see the prosecutors about cooperating the day after I had my meeting. We had barely beat him to the punch. While things do not always work out so lopsidedly well for cooperators, this is an example of why, with a little luck, this route can be so appealing.

The impetus to cooperate is also an element in the reduced numbers of trials, especially in multi-defendant cases. Non-cooperating defendants must now, more often than ever, have to deal with the trial testimony of a cooperating insider. Insiders can corroborate what the government already knows, and can potentially reveal additional facts that can produce even more damaging evidence than was the basis for the original charges.

For those of us who have regularly tried cases over the decades, there is an additional, yet significant, reason for the steep reduction in the number of federal cases that actually go to trial. Simply put, it is often meaningfully harder from an evidentiary point of view to successfully defend criminal cases today than, say, 40 years ago.

As previously noted, the federal government has always been the heavy favorite at trial for any number of reasons. First, there is the issue of deep pockets. I have been fortunate to have represented many wealthy clients over the years, but none had the budget of the Department of Justice. Second, prosecutors have extraordinarily broad subpoena power to compel people, documents, and physical evidence before a grand jury. They also have at their disposal highly skilled federal agents, principally from the IRS and FBI, to help build really solid cases. Finally, subject to rare statute of limitations issues, time is on the government's side. Indictments are not actually filed until a case has been made as airtight as possible. If the case cannot be made as strong as necessary, an indictment will rarely emerge.

This has always been the reality. What is new is technology.

When I earlier described the trial brilliance of Jimmy LaRossa, I identified him as the first defense lawyer to beat me as a prosecutor. He and the also-praised Jerry Lewis got acquittals in my fourth trial, the prosecution of fringe organized crime figures charged with thefts of cargo from JFK airport terminals. The core of my case was the testimony of a cargo handler caught helping the defendants in one aspect of their operation. The balance of my presentation was comprised of little things that tended to corroborate his version of events, such as customs documents and bills of lading. Jimmy and Jerry destroyed the cargo handler on cross and the case was lost.

That kind of "bare bones" case would not be brought today.

Particularly in today's white collar world, defense attorneys must confront either tape recordings of their client and/or his confederates discussing, or even actually committing the crime, devastating emails taken from his or a co-defendant's hard drive, cell phone records, GPS data, or some combination thereof. Confronted with such often damning evidence, defendants in criminal cases and their attorneys must face the harsh reality that technology has made going to trial far riskier than it would otherwise be.

For the attorneys, that reality looms over much more than any individual case. It now looms over a career, something that takes a great deal of time and effort to create. The term "disruptive technologies" is generally associated with the effects on blue collar jobs, such as robots replacing factory workers. While technology is surely something less than "disruptive" in the courtroom context, it nonetheless can directly impact an attorney's ability to defend certain white collar criminal cases.

An example. Some years ago, I was in a highly publicized political corruption prosecution in the Southern District of New York before Judge Rakoff. New York State Senator Carl Kruger was the lead defendant, represented by Ben Brafman. Ben brought me in to represent a close Kruger associate, Dr. Michael Turano. Among the others indicted were two businessmen with ties to Senator Kruger, represented by Andrew Lawler and Gerald Lefcourt. Andy and Gerry each enjoyed very substantial and well-deserved reputations in the New York white collar community (and Lefcourt, one of the original "Chicago Seven" attorneys, a national reputation). While I had worked closely with both Andy and Gerry on any number of matters over the years, I had not actually tried a case with either.

As the four of us worked together in the months preceding the trial, and the elements of our coordinated defense began fitting into place, I eagerly looked forward to being on trial with Ben, Andy, and Gerry in what promised to be a great experience. This was especially the case with a judge like Rakoff, who, as a prominent prosecutor and defense lawyer before taking the bench, recognized and appreciated the work of skilled attorneys appearing before him. The pending trial promised to be something special.

It never happened.

Instead, as we got closer to trial we received more and more "discovery" material from the government, that is, much of what the prosecution's trial evidence would be. Among the discovery materials were emails and surreptitious, undercover tape recordings made during the investigation of the political corruption scheme alleged in the indictment. One of the tapes devastatingly impacted an important element of our defense. The net result was that going to trial, notwithstanding the skill of the defense team, became much too risky. All clients ended up pleading guilty.

While there are surely other things that may have contributed to the vanishing trial, such as a decline in specific crime rates over the years, I believe the main culprit and its junior partner are as identified.

So, how does the scarcity of trials and the resulting decline in the number of defense attorneys with the skill level that only extensive trial experience can bring, impact defendants' rights?

The Sixth Amendment to the U.S. Constitution guarantees, among other things, that criminal defendants have the right to counsel, which necessarily includes the right to "the effective assistance of counsel." The Supreme Court has employed a two-pronged test to define effective assistance: first, the defendant must prove the lawyer's courtroom performance fell below "an objective standard of reasonableness, and that counsel's sub-standard performance prejudiced the defendant." Prejudice is defined as the "reasonable probability that but for counsel's unprofessional errors, the result of the proceeding would have been different."

More recently, lower courts have concluded that the effective assistance standard applies beyond courtroom performance, to also encompass counseling a defendant whether to take a guilty plea or go to trial. One commentator explained the underlying logic as follows. "Given the longer sentences that modern criminal adjudication imposes on defendants who choose trial and lose, effective assistance is necessary to ensure that this choice, like the choice to accept a plea bargain, is voluntary and intelligent."

The problem with both the case law on effective assistance of counsel and the scholarly analysis of the same is that neither address the current reality that there are fewer and fewer lawyers with the battle-tested level of experience necessary to defeat criminal charges at a trial in federal court. Historically, federal prosecutors have won the overwhelming percentage of cases they try, and that history includes the decades before the Sentencing Guidelines came into effect, when there was no shortage of skilled and seasoned defense attorneys. Today, while those lawyers with rusted or mediocre skills (and less) will surely be able to perform above the low "effectiveness of counsel" standard, such skills are hardly sufficient to achieve successful results, especially in light of the scientific and technical advances that have only enhanced the prosecutorial arsenal.

A host of interrelated, unanswerable questions are raised.

Does the defendant's choice to go trial or take a plea include a realistic assessment of the attorney's actual courtroom skills? A client's ability to know in advance just how capable his or her lawyer actually is in the courtroom has always been an open question. Now, however, the conundrum is exacerbated by the fact that the odds of selecting a truly talented courtroom performer have been materially reduced because relatively fewer battle-tested performers are still available. In situations where the trial attorney's ability has been reduced by a lack of real trial experience, does that fact force a guilty plea in a case that would otherwise go to trial with a more skilled attorney? Can the lawyer without real trial experience recognize the opportunities for courtroom victory? Even if he or she is able to do so, does that lawyer, aware of his or her inability to capitalize, recommend pleading guilty in order to keep the case and earn a fee? In sum, the new reality has put those charged with criminal conduct on the federal level in increasing peril.

Absent a significant modification of the Sentencing Guidelines, it is difficult to expect a resurgence of trials.

Certain potential improvements, such as lowering total sentencing ranges and restoring the mandatory service of one-third
of the sentence imposed, down from the present 85 percent, come
readily to mind. While a full discussion of potential improvements
is well beyond the purpose of this book, there is surely an ample
supply of legal scholars, judges and lawyers who are well-qualified
to remediate the situation.

That said, the fact remains that although the modifications
introduced over the years have certainly made the Guidelines less
onerous, they have had no real impact on the vanishing trial and
the attendant consequences of that phenomenon. Accordingly, the
simplest and best approach might be to admit the Guidelines have
been a failure and eliminate them entirely, reverting to the system
in place before trials started to disappear. Given political realities,
such a major admission of legislative error is not likely.

Whatever the best remedy turns out to be, it will never be
implemented without a meaningful degree of public awareness to
overcome the power of elected officials still caught up in the "lock
'em up" mindset that helped create this situation in the first place.
Surely, they and their political backers, the corporations that build
and operate prisons, and the poor, rural communities that depend
on prisons to provide local employment, will not just go away. Thus,
unless and until public awareness of the vanishing trial and its consequences is substantially increased, it is difficult to expect real change.

The public must refuse to be shut out of the most powerful and
important component of our criminal justice system: the federal
courts. It must insist on preserving its constitutionally mandated
role in federal criminal trials, and not allow the process to become
an assembly line operated by unelected professionals, in Judge Ra-

koff's words, "behind closed doors." Politicians must hear from their constituents that it is better for district court judges to exercise their sound discretion in sentencing defendants than forcing them to follow numerical formulas calculated to imprison more people for longer terms; that real prison reform is a "front-burner" priority; that senators and congressmen who continue to reflect the "law and order" mentality will no longer be supported; and that only candidates seeking meaningful sentencing reform will get their votes.

That public pressure can produce significant criminal justice reform is exemplified by the November 2019 release of 527 non-violent offenders from Oklahoma jails. Oklahoma was a leader among states that embraced the "lock 'em up" approach that dominated the political landscape starting in the 1980s. By 2015 it had the highest per capita prison population in the country. Ultimately, the conclusion of a leading Republican state legislator that, "over-incarceration is the definition of inefficient government, producing neither increased safety nor less crime," became a widely accepted fact. In 2016, two ballot initiatives reclassifying certain low-level felonies as misdemeanors passed overwhelmingly, leading to the prisoner release. The cost savings to taxpayers is estimated to be some 11.9 million dollars.

Confronting the dangers posed by the vanishing trial requires a nationwide outcry directed at our federal criminal justice system. The minimal attention paid thus far has led to correspondingly minimal results. For example, the recent, trumpeted, "First Step" sentencing reform bill, is, unfortunately, only a small initial step. Its provisions, including more equitable punishment for drug offenders, expanded job training programs to reduce recidivism, and making sure that more prisoners serve time in jails near their families, while laudable, will have zero impact on the decision to go to trial.

Fairness can only be restored when major reform is achieved, and the ill-conceived Sentencing Guidelines regimen that substitutes arbitrary mathematics for sound judicial discretion is either drastically redesigned or completely abandoned. Brutal disincentives to going to trial will be removed when deserving inmates can return to society after serving a reasonable portion of a reasonable sentence, and not an arbitrarily high 85 percent of an unnecessarily long sentence.

But even if the Guidelines are meaningfully and appropriately changed or even eliminated, won't technology still be with us? Shouldn't we expect that the future will bring even more intrusive and powerful technologies? Yet, don't we want and need technologies and scientific advances like DNA to identify the guilty? Doesn't the government have not only the right, but the obligation to present its most powerful admissible evidence? Of course. That said, the important and increasing role of tech-based evidence only underscores the need for experienced and talented trial lawyers.

Often, conversations caught on tape can be misleading, and cryptic remarks made in emails or tweets can be especially obtuse. A case in point. In the late 1990s I represented a young investment banker under investigation by the U.S. Securities and Exchange Commission. We were confronted with a seemingly damaging set of email correspondence he had with another investment banker. The SEC lawyers, understandably, viewed the email exchanges in the light most negative, and were preparing charges.

As it turns out, the actual meaning of these emails was quite different than a literal reading suggested. My client was born and raised in Lahore, Pakistan, and came to the U.S. to attend Princeton. The emails were with his closest childhood friend, a Pakistani who also came to the U.S. to attend college and launch a career.

The emails were loaded with the personal jargon and cynical irony unique to their relationship. Once explained and put in proper context, they were hardly the incriminating communications the SEC believed them to be.

In the courtroom, it is with this type of tech-based evidence that on its face is "un-cross examinable," that the abilities of an experienced, talented trial lawyer are simply irreplaceable. It is ironic that the emergence of technology as a significant factor leading to the dearth of trial experience is also an important reason why such experience is more vital now than ever.

The combination of the Federal Sentencing Guidelines and the increasingly significant impact of technology has brought us to where we are now. We desperately need to change what we must of the former, so that able defense lawyers can effectively deal with the latter.

Time is not an ally. A 2017 Jeffrey Toobin *New Yorker* piece, a second, rare example of the discussion about the "vanishing trial" for the general public, addresses the time-sensitive nature of the problem. The article profiles Ben Brafman as "The Last of the Big Time Defense Attorneys" and examines the dearth of criminal trials (and, inferentially, big-time criminal trial lawyers) that has become the new reality.

Toobin writes, "Traditionally, trial lawyering has been a game for young men (and historically, it's been mostly men), and Brafman is well aware that many of his mentors and peers, like Jimmy LaRossa and Gustave Newman, have passed from the scene." Ben, while acknowledging the "passing of the years," promises to slow down a bit, but vows to continue. He asks, "What else am I going to do?"

As long as the present paucity of federal criminal trials continues, fewer and fewer young lawyers will develop real trial skills, and the abilities of courtroom veterans will continue to rust, all while the remaining old pros retire or pass away. The question Ben Brafman asks about himself can be adapted and projected onto our federal criminal justice system itself. Without an ample supply of skilled courtroom lawyers, what is the criminal justice system going to do?

CHAPTER EIGHTEEN

SUMMING UP

Near the end of 2012, I was asked a startling question by a young associate in a large law firm. His firm's client and mine were both targets of a federal grand jury investigation, and over the months as our two teams worked closely together to coordinate the defense, he and I had developed something of a mentor/mentee relationship. He had been with his firm almost four years at the time, had an impressive academic background, and was beginning to think of career options. At lunch one day in a conversation about the differences between his generation and mine, he asked me to look back over the decades and identify the single smartest career decision I had ever made. Needless to say, I was a bit taken aback. After a pause I replied, "Deciding to be born in 1946."

What I meant was that fate, as much as talent, dedication, or intelligence, was a key element in the fortunate career that I had. I was lucky enough to have entered adulthood at a time of expanding horizons in the United States, a time of great opportunity for young people, especially white males. Growing up in a middle-class family in Queens, New York, I had goals my parents set for me; goals

I internalized. If I could meet those targets, while there was no guarantee, I could create a reliable path for moving up in the world.

Principal among these objectives was that I graduate high school with at least an 88 average to qualify for the City University of New York's senior colleges. Magically, I graduated Andrew Jackson High School with a GPA of exactly 88. I chose Brooklyn College over CUNY's Queens College because going to Queens would have meant taking one of the same buses I took to high school; going to Brooklyn forced my father to get me a car. Put another way, Brooklyn was as far out of town as I could get.

While I had certainly heard of the Ivy League, I had not heard much. There was no need to focus on anything beyond City University's four senior colleges, not only because they were all we could afford, but just as important, because of their well-deserved academic reputations, they were all I needed.

My ignorance of elite educational institutions is revealed in the following story. In my first year of law school, a classmate with whom I was becoming friendly told me that he had gone to "Penn." In subsequently introducing him to another classmate, I said that he had attended "Penn State." He could not hide his anger in correcting me, pointing out that he had gone to "Penn, not Penn State." I had no idea why he was so unhappy. Fact was, I had never heard of the University of Pennsylvania, but I knew Penn State because of its football team. My ignorance of scholastic status turned him off and our friendship never really got off the ground. Things got even chillier between us when I made Law Review and he did not.

I reached the academic goal that all of my first-year classmates shared because I received a superb education at Brooklyn College, where the competition was fierce and the academics first-rate. The price? The student fee/tuition was $32.00 a term. When the fee went to nearly $60.00 there were student protests and picketing at Boylan Hall, the school's administration building. You still had to purchase textbooks of course, but working in the Brooklyn College Bookstore gave me a substantial discount.

When over the years the burdensome cost of college came up in conversation with others of my generation, I would often say that it cost me far more to send my oldest child on his tour of potential colleges than it cost my parents to send me to college. Law school was affordable to my middle-class family because of much more modest tuition levels and a generous trustee fellowship. While competition for federal clerkships and federal prosecutor positions was only slightly less brutal "back in the day," positioning oneself for potential selection was much more egalitarian. As important, if and when you achieved your desired career goal there were no burdensome student loans to pay off. How would I have handled the payments? I earned $11,800 the year I clerked for Judge Gasch.

What I also had in mind with my typically cynical reply to my young friend was that I was able to become a trial lawyer at a time when the road to develop the skills necessary to try cases at the highest level was a four-lane freeway, and the value of those skills was beyond question. There is good reason to fear that road may now be a single, expensive toll lane and the ultimate destination has become much less alluring.

Will the next young lawyer with the rare, inherent talent and drive to become a Milton Gould, Pat Tuite, or Ben Brafman have the necessary institutional ecosystem in which to develop and hone that ability? Will that ability be as fundamentally important to our criminal justice system and so highly prized?

There is no law school equivalent of performing arts institutions such as New York's Juilliard, where attendance is based on

talent, talent that can be evaluated in advance of, and as a prerequisite to, admission. Law schools primarily focus on an applicant's
academics, and a narrow aspect of academic ability at that. Although
each of the trial lawyers lauded in this book was and is really smart,
their intellect was neither oriented toward the legal scholarship and
analysis required for success in law school, nor was that type of
intellect necessary to their later courtroom success.

What was essential was their innate and abundant talent as
performance artists, a skill set that could only emerge after law
school and be developed only with years of meaningful experience
in the courtroom. Francis Wellman, in his landmark treatise, *The
Art of Cross-Examination*, put it squarely more than a century ago
in arguing that trials should be conducted only by trial specialists
who work in the courtroom every day, not by lawyers known in his
time as general practitioners. "It is experience, and one might say
experience alone, that brings success."

The talent of the courtroom giants cited in this book could only
emerge in a real-world environment that provided one trial experience after another, year in and year out. The abundance of federal
trials and the exalted status afforded to the top federal trial lawyers
provided both the environment and the incentive to emerge as the
polished and accomplished professionals they ultimately became.

In today's federal criminal justice system with so few trials, how
will the past generation's potential progeny get that elite level of
experience? What reward awaits someone who possesses a skill set
so infrequently in demand? At least when Henry Ford's "horseless
carriage" arrived at the turn of the twentieth century, blacksmiths
making horseshoes became relics of the past to society's substantial
benefit. If the present dearth of trials means that tomorrow's federal
trial lawyers somehow become an updated version of yesterday's

blacksmiths, it is difficult to see the upside to society.

Of the many obvious downsides, of course, the most devastating is the virtual elimination of the average citizen's vital role in the administration of criminal justice on the country's most important level.

I am mindful, of course, that older generations tend to view the past in a romanticized way, looking back to see their own era as a "golden age" of one kind or another. That is hardly surprising, as the past was when today's elderly were young and vibrant; a time when today's septuagenarians and octogenarians did not have to spend 15 minutes each day just looking for their glasses.

I still recall a remark made many years ago by a friend of my father during a conversation we were having about music. He said, "They stopped making good music by the 1960s." As a child of the 60s, I found the remark to be particularly ludicrous. While I chose not to respond directly, there were many things to say. If in referring to "they" he meant George Gershwin, Oscar Hammerstein, and Jimmy Dorsey, he was correct, as by the early 1960s those giants were, sadly, no longer alive to make their music. But, of course, by "they" he meant all musicians and songwriters. This is because he was oblivious to the torrent of brilliant music of all types produced in the 1960s and the decades to follow. As the old wisecrack goes, "Just because you never heard of the Civil War does not mean there wasn't one." While I like to think that my generation is at least somewhat more aware of current culture, the fact that I loved the play *Hamilton* hardly means I have a real understanding or a genuine appreciation of hip-hop music (or is it rap?).

However wrongheaded my father's friend's declaration comparing the past in which he had so immersed himself, to the present he ignored, we thankfully have available to us much of the recorded music from the era he so justifiably cherished. Sadly, we have no videos to watch Jerry Lewis, shiny, black toupee akimbo, summing up in Brooklynese, or to capture the baritone Jimmy LaRossa strutting around the courtroom with all eyes glued on him as he cross-examines a witness who would rather be anywhere else on the planet.

To whatever degree impacted by nostalgia, or containing recollections of events which are, to quote Nora Ephron, "subject to interpretation," this book is an attempt to preserve to at least some material degree, the essence of the courtroom era that was, so more of us can appreciate what is being lost. Far less complete, compelling, or aesthetically beautiful than a digitalized version of "Rhapsody in Blue," or the latest Broadway revival of Porgy and Bess, it can hopefully contribute to a much-needed public discussion of how to preserve the vital role jurors and skilled trial lawyers play in maintaining the fundamental fairness of our federal criminal justice system.

That discussion cannot come soon enough. To borrow a phrase from Bob Dylan, "The hour is getting late."

The vanishing trial and the resulting passing of the era of courtroom performers has sobering implications. Like the loss of the oceans' coral reefs, the ongoing disappearance of federal criminal trials signals an increasing imbalance in our nation's criminal justice ecosystem that must not be ignored.

EPILOGUE

I write this book from my home office in a beach community in Southern California, where my wife and I now live. After 39 years of practicing law together, Ken Kaplan and I closed our New York City boutique white collar criminal firm, Kaplan & Katzberg, on December 31, 2015. I have often described the firm's fortunate run in the following way—we did the right thing, by and large, for the wrong reasons. By that I meant that, when we left the United States Attorney's Office in February 1977, we believed we had the necessary relationships to attract clients and maintain a practice. Lawyers are professionals, of course, but private practice lawyers are also business people. It is one thing to have the training, skill set, and experience to do the legal work on a high enough level; it is quite another to have actual clients to pay you for providing these services. The previously mentioned Bill Shea of Shea & Gould is not famous for his lawyering, but his ability to generate torrents of business made him essential to the firm's success.

As it turned out, the people and circumstances Ken and I had originally believed would provide a client referral base turned out to be more wishful thinking than accurate prognosis. Fortunately, people we had not yet met and circumstances we could never have imagined, formed the basis of a business that endured almost four decades.

In *The Operator*, a biography of the music and movie mogul David Geffen, the late Tom King tells the story of a dinner held in honor of Ahmet Ertegun, a pioneering, hugely successful music producer and entrepreneur, who was an early Geffen mentor. In his remarks accepting the accolades of the dinner's attendees, Ertegun said that he is often asked the secret of his success. The secret he said (and I paraphrase), is to walk down the street very slowly, until you bump into someone who will make you rich and successful. While I assume this line got the laughs Ertegun expected, I was struck by the inherent wisdom lurking within this seemingly self-deprecating remark.

Acknowledging the incredibly random nature of life is, of course, crucial to recognizing how things come to be. Like the old saying goes, "Rule One, be lucky. Rule Two, see Rule One." But Ertegun's formula for success actually contains three additional elements. The first is patience, as indicated by the need to walk down the street very slowly. The two others are inherent in the story, an ability to recognize the person you have just met by chance as a potentially important ally, teacher, or supporter, and the need to respond to that person accordingly.

I will never know how many people I have bumped into on the street of my career and mistakenly took them for pickpockets, when they were actually persons who could have helped me in any number of ways. Given my admittedly unfortunate "all or nothing" view of most people, I am sure the list is long. At least I was lucky enough to have recognized how much both Ken Kaplan and Ben Brafman would add to my personal and professional well-being when I bumped into them.

But at 69 years of age, and with two of three adult children, their spouses, and (most importantly) all four grandchildren living in Southern California, the time for change had arrived. When surprised colleagues asked why I was heading for the left coast, I would tell them that Leslie and I found it too difficult to sufficiently spoil the grandkids from 3,000 miles away. Joking aside, I knew I was leaving professional and personal relationships that could not be duplicated. Yet, it was time to move on.

In writing this book, the distance from my New York career, a result of both geography and, more importantly, the passage of time, while surely imposing limits on my capacity to reconstruct, has brought benefits as well. It has allowed me to reflect on aspects of my career that I had either not focused on or fully appreciated at the time. A person can look back upon the same event at different times in his or her life and have a different, yet meaningful, takeaway each time.

That reality was driven home to me many years ago after Leslie and I watched the Luis Bunuel movie, *Belle de Jour*. It features the beautiful Catherine Deneuve as a wealthy, aristocratic, Parisian woman who tries to address her strong, internal conflicts by becoming a prostitute. I had originally seen the movie when it came out in 1967. I was 21 years old, and the sight of Catherine Deneuve, in her prime and in her underwear, disrupted my central nervous system for weeks thereafter. *Belle de Jour* was re-released on its 25th anniversary and I saw it again, as a middle-aged, married man. I left the theater dazzled once again, but this time by the exquisite French antiques in her luxurious apartment, objects I had somehow missed the first time around.

In reporting on the vanishing trial, I have attempted to use the distance between now and then to reflect upon what once was;

to focus on all experiences, including those I may have given little attention to at the time, and thus, meaningfully recreate both the day-to-day reality, and the emotional power of courtroom life "back in the day."

Finally, I am still practicing law. Thanks to a long, close relationship with Bill Sharp—an acclaimed, international tax lawyer whom I had the good fortune to "bump into" later in my career—I have my present role, as consulting counsel to Holland & Knight, a stellar, global, law firm. It allows me to be more selective in my caseload while still working with really top-flight lawyers. Whether I ever try another case is an open question.

With my grandson, Dax, at the beach,
September 2017.

NOTES

CHAPTER ONE

Page 2 — Table 5.5, "U.S. District Courts, Criminal Defendants Disposed of, by Method of Disposition," 2011 Annual Report by the Director of Judicial Business; Table D-4, "U.S. Courts, Federal Judicial Caseload Statistics," Updated March 31, 2018. www.uscourts. gov/statistics-reports/federal-judicial-caseload-statistics-2018. The latest statistics are even worse. In fiscal year 2018, the number of federal defendants who went to trial dropped to 2 percent. Pew Research, "FactTank," June 11, 2019, https://www.pewresearch. org/fact-tank/2019/06/11only-2-of-federal-criminal-defendants-go-to-trial-and-most-who-do-are-found-guilty.

The reports do not reflect the total number of charged misdemeanor offenses. Misdemeanors, for which there is no right to trial by jury, comprise a very small percentage of federal criminal charges. Thus, if they are an undisclosed subset of these reports, it would only marginally change the calculation. In either event, the steep, ongoing decline in the number of jury trials would remain the same.

Page 3 — Benjamin Weiser, "Trial by Jury, a Hallowed American Right, is Vanishing," *The New York Times*, August 7, 2016. https://www.nytimes.com/nyregion/jury-trials-vanish-and-justice-isserved-behind-closed-doors.html.

———

Patricia Lee Refo, "The Vanishing Trial," *Litigation*, Volume 30, Number 2, page 2, Winter 2004. http://www.abanet.otg/litigation/home.html

Page 6 — Nora Ephron's play, *Lucky Guy*, had its Broadway premier on April 1, 2013 at the Broadhurst Theater.

CHAPTER TWO

Page 9 — I am hardly the only one born in the 1940s to have "done better" than their parents. As Michael Lewis reports in his book *The Fifth Risk*, more than 90 percent of children born in 1940 went on to earn more than their parents. Only half of those born in the 1980s did so. *The Fifth Risk*, W.W. Norton and Company, 2018 at page 177.

For me, doing "better than my father" was the result of a combination of disparate benefits conferred upon my generation, advantages bestowed by serendipity, not by talent, or even hard work. I was able to obtain a first-rate college education at CUNY's Brooklyn College at virtually no cost (see, Chapter Eighteen); I started earning substantial sums of money in the early 1980s right at the time Ronald Reagan began to meaningfully reduce the federal income tax on higher incomes; timely additions to the tax code like IRAs, 401(k) accounts, and defined benefit plans, allowed me to put away a large portion of my income each year, deduct that sum from my taxable income, and let that money grow, tax-free, over the decades until retirement; finally, I needed to purchase a home in the late 1970s after my two sons were born, just as housing prices were in the early stage of a dramatic, four decades-long, price increase.

CHAPTER THREE

Pages 14–15 — It is only recently that law school pedigree is being looked at in a completely analytic, algorithmic way, as compared to the traditional elitist perspective that has prevailed for many decades. This new, data-centric approach challenges fundamental assumptions about elite legal institutions. For example, a prominent statistical analyst reports that the correlation between an attorney's law school and his or her eventual success in the legal profession is zero, that is, the law school one attends "does not matter at all." Malcom Gladwell, *Revisionist History*, Season 4, episodes 1 and 2.

Page 23 — Given how the concert, billed as the "West Coast Woodstock," turned out, the Stones and all participants would have wished that Belli had failed to convince local authorities to permit the event. The show's producers somehow believed it was a good idea to have the Hells Angels provide security, and that adequate infrastructure, including a sufficient number of toilets, was not necessary. A madhouse ensued, causing one of the featured bands, The Grateful Dead, to refuse to perform. Ultimately four people died, including a black, 18-year-old fan, Murdock Hunter, who was stabbed to death by a Hells Angel during the Stones' performance. https://www.washingtonpost.com/graphics/2019/lifestyle/altamont-rolling-stones-50th-anniversary/

CHAPTER FOUR

Page 32 — United States v. Nazarro, 472 F.2d 302 (2d Cir.) 1973.

In reviewing Judge Rosling's pro-prosecution interference in the trial of James Nazarro, Second Circuit Judge Irving Kaufman, speaking for a unanimous panel, wrote:

"Rarely is there a case reaching us after conviction in which the defendant believes he has received a fair trial. The human tendency to blame a trial judge for the jury's verdict is a frailty we often encounter, and almost as frequently we find such claims to be without merit or substance. Once again we are asked by a convicted defendant to consider a claim of improper conduct on the part of the trial judge. In this instance, however, we believe the record amply demonstrates that the defendant did not receive a fair trial." <u>United States v. Nazarro</u>, 472 F. 2d 302, 303 (2d Cir. 1973).

CHAPTER FIVE

Page 36 — When Bill Shea died in 1991, his obituary in *The New York Times* was headlined, "The Lawyer Behind the Mets." It reported that Shea bragged he "never really practiced law in the conventional sense," and that people in his office "jokingly speculated whether he even knew where the courthouse was." *The New York Times*, October 4, 1991; https://www.nytimes.com/1991/10/04/nyregion/William-a-shea-84-dies-the-lawyer-behind-the-mets.

Page 37 — Edward R. Korman, now a senior judge, was appointed to the Eastern District of New York bench by President Reagan in 1985. An honors graduate of both Brooklyn College and Brooklyn Law School, he began his legal career as a law clerk to Chief Judge Kenneth Keating of the New York Court of Appeals, and then entered private practice with Paul Weiss Rifkin Wharton & Garrison in 1968. Judge Korman left Paul Weiss in 1972 to serve as an Assistant Solicitor General of the United States, representing the federal government before the Supreme Court. He was the Chief Assistant United States Attorney for the Eastern District of New York from 1974–1978, and United States Attorney from 1978-1982. Judge Korman returned to private practice as a partner at Stroock & Stroock & Lavan until his appointment to the bench. He is the recipient of the Federal Bar Council's Learned Hand Medal for Excellence and the New York County Lawyers' Association Edward Weinfeld Award. While Judge Korman is perhaps best known for his handling of complex Holocaust reparation litigation, his scholarly judicial opinions have often been singled out for special praise. As a prime example, Linda Greenhouse, legal scholar, Yale Law School professor, and *New York Times* Contributing Opinion Writer, in her review of Judge Korman's ruling in a litigation involving Obamacare contraception regulations, wrote this. "If you read only one judicial opinion this year, you might consider skipping the Supreme Court entirely and going right to a decision issued earlier this month by Judge Edward R. Korman of Federal District Court in Brooklyn." Linda Greenhouse, "Of Judges and Judging," *The New York Times*, April 17, 2013. http://opiniator. blogs. nytimes.com/2013/04/17/of-judges-and-judging/?src=rechp. Full disclosure: Ed Korman is a personal friend.

CHAPTER SIX

Page 45 — *The Manhattan Lawyer*, then a leading, weekly publication in the New York legal community, ran a feature article on the Marty Solomon case titled, "Ex-Officer of Citisource Recalls a 3-Year Nightmare." It detailed Solomon's financial and emotional suffering during our prolonged resistance to pressure from Southern District of New York prosecutors. While he labeled me a "hero," Marty openly expressed his ongoing anger and bitterness at what he called a "merciless" government. The article described me as "more matter of fact" about the tactics prosecutors employed, saying, "I don't think it's illegal or unethical. It's basic All-American hardball. But it's a hardball league." *The Manhattan Lawyer,* S2, Volume 2, No. 21, February 14-20, 1989.

CHAPTER SEVEN

Pages 52–53 — The limited role of counsel in the federal jury selection process is not mandated by statute or procedural rule. That said, whatever its genesis, it is the overwhelming norm. In this regard, I checked with a number of experienced federal trial lawyers, both prosecutors and defense attorneys. They were able to cite only a small number of exceptions, mainly judges who, after conducting an initial, standard *voir dire*, allowed attorneys to pose a limited number of follow-up questions through the court, or directly to the jury.

Page 56 — Tom Petty, "The Waiting," Warner Chappel Music, 1981.

Josh Gerstein, Darren Samuelsohn, "Manafort Trial Day 15: Jury goes home without a verdict," *Politico,* August 20, 2018; ttps://www.politico.com/story/2018/08/20/manafort-trial-jury-trump-justice-788491.

Page 57 — I have found it much less difficult to deal with the stress involved in the sentencing of a client after he or she pleaded guilty than the anxiety involved in waiting for a jury verdict. It is easier (not easy) since most often you have recommended the plea deal because you have fashioned it to minimize the client's exposure, and the Federal Sentencing Guidelines let you and the client know with a degree of certainty what the maximum and minimum sentences can be. As a result, although you are obviously traversing deadly serious, negative terrain, it is a landscape of identifiable shades of gray, unlike the black and white, all or nothing, jury's verdict of guilt or innocence.

For the client being sentenced, however, the pressure of whether you are going to jail, and if so, for how long, can be brutal. Will you be around to be with your spouse and children? If not, how long will you be away? How will you handle the stress of incarceration? What emotional harm will be caused to the loved ones you are leaving behind? These and a host of other questions, including financial, family, and career anxieties, leave many clients in psychic purgatory from the day they take a plea, until weeks later when they are sentenced.

Ben Brafman, a courtroom star featured in Chapter Nine, recently shared an incident with me that starkly reveals this distress. During a brief trip he made to Los Angeles, we enjoyed an extended poolside breakfast at his hotel. One of the many topics covered was the emotional stress of Ben's high-profile career. It triggered a recollection of a client he had many years ago, and his sentencing in a white collar case. With Ben's permission, and a few, small edits in the description of the client to guarantee his/her confidentiality, the incident is recounted below.

The client was a very emotional man with a large family and a private business on the brink of collapse. He was facing somewhere between 12 and 18 months under the Federal Sentencing Guidelines. Ben had moved for a "downward departure" that, if granted, would allow the client to be sentenced to probation, and thus avoid jail. On the day of the sentence, the client was a nervous wreck, dripping with perspiration. During the long and painful sentencing hearing, Ben noticed that the client's right hand was always clenched in a fist.

Fortunately, the judge gave the client probation. In the joyful hugs that followed their exit from the courtroom, Ben saw that the client's right fist remained clinched. He asked the man what was in his hand. The client spread his fingers to expose a capsule. It was cyanide, which the client intended to swallow immediately if sentenced to prison.

CHAPTER EIGHT

Page 62 — As reported in the media, my cross-examination of Tyco's general counsel, Brian Moroze, focused on numerous, similar (albeit smaller) loans Tyco had made to other executives and employees, thus making the Belnick loan "normal" and "appropriate." Objections to this line of questioning were overruled by the court. Christopher Mumma, "Defense Says Ex-Tyco Lawyer's Loan was Normal," *The Washington Post*, May 18, 2004. Http://www.washingtonpost.com/wpdyn/articles/A35591-2004May18.html.

Page 65 — Mark Belnick has remained an active participant in the law, including his ongoing role as adjunct professor of constitutional law at Princeton University. At the same time, he has enjoyed a successful acting career, recently starring in the Los Angeles production of Arthur Miller's play *All My Sons*.

Courtroom sketch on page 67 — Cameras are not allowed in federal court, nor in most state courts. In high publicity cases, media outlets employ artists to make courtroom drawings to be used in television reports, or purchase the work of "free agent" artists who sell their work to television stations. Lawyers in these cases often purchase the drawings (if they are prominent enough in the picture), or copies of same, frame them, and hang them on an office wall. Predictably, the big name trial lawyers accumulated quite a bit of courtroom art over their careers. Jay Goldberg, discussed in Chapter Fourteen, had so many such drawings that they covered the walls on both sides of the long hallway leading to his corner office, high above Park Avenue.

CHAPTER NINE

Page 70 — Judge Ellis's repeated confrontations with prosecutors included a direction to Mr. Andres not to "look down" when the judge criticized him. Andres, a seasoned and highly regarded former Eastern District of New York prosecutor, held both his tongue and his ground. That Mr. Andres was able to successfully deal with a federal judge should hardly come as a surprise, because in addition to his substantial courtroom experience, he is married to Ronnie Abrams, a judge in the Southern District of New York. A more comprehensive look at Judge Ellis' confrontational conduct in the Manafort trial can be found at https://www.nytimes.com/2018/08/09/us/politics/judge-ellis-manafort-trial.html.

Page 71 – *The New York Times* obituary for Judge Platt, outlining his career, can be found at: https://www.nytimes.com/2017/03/06/nyregion/thomas-platt-judge-who-fined-striking-air-traffic-controllers-dies. html

Page 72 — John Prine, *Dear Abby*, A & R, 1973.

Page 74 — A brief word about trial transcripts.

All criminal proceedings include official reporters, employed by the court, who take verbatim, stenographic notes. The notes will be used to create an actual transcript of a particular proceeding only if the judge, or either of the parties, orders one. The reporter charges the parties a set price per page. There are two types of orders—daily copy and regular. Daily copy is ordered when a party needs a transcript to use the next day, either in that proceeding, or for a filing based upon the proceeding. Court reporters charge a higher price per page for the expedited service. Regular orders can take weeks to fulfill, depending on any number of variables, unnecessary to this discussion.

That I do not have the transcript of many of the trials discussed in this book reflects either: that a transcript in the matter was never ordered; one was ordered, but ultimately forwarded to the client; or, a transcript was ordered and kept in Kaplan & Katzberg's closed case files, and ultimately shredded in the normal course of the firm's record retention policy.

Page 82 — Mark A. Costantino was elevated from Staten Island Civil Court to the federal bench by President Nixon in 1971. The sports equivalent would be going from a Division Three college baseball team to the major leagues. In 1973, unspecified allegations of wrongdoing and governmental accusations of ineptitude produced talk of impeachment. A judicial counsel of the Second Circuit Court of Appeals investigated, but took no action. Judge Costantino retired from active service in 1987.

Pages 87–88 — Margaret A. Jacobs, "'Were You Alone or by Yourself?' And Other Courtroom Gaffes," *The Wall Street Journal*, June 15, 1998. https://wwwwsj.com/articles/SB89786003677945500.

Pages 88–90 — *Kramer vs. Kramer*, Columbia Pictures, 1979.

Page 96 — Two separate polls, one of judges, one of lawyers, taken by *The Chicago Lawyer* in 1988 ranked Pat Tuite the top defense lawyer in Chicago. In 1991, *The National Law Journal* called him one of the nation's best criminal defense lawyers. https://www.chicagotribune. com/news/ctxpm-1993-08-24-9308240183-story. html. Pat Tuite is now retired and lives in Florida.

Page 98 — A few years later, Marvin Glass pleaded guilty to unrelated racketeering and tax fraud charges, arising from his defrauding clients out of large sums of money. A brief summary of that prosecution can be found in a *Chicago Tribune* article dated May 20,

1986. https://www.chicagotribune.com/news/ct-xpm-1986-05-20-8602060186-story.html.

CHAPTER ELEVEN

Page 109 — *The Hill*, https://the hill.com/homenews/media/324834survey-only-43-percent-can-name-a-supreme-court-justice.

Page 110 — John G. Roberts was appointed a Supreme Court Associate Justice by President George W. Bush in 2005. When Chief Justice William Rehnquist died before Roberts was confirmed, President Bush nominated him to be Chief Justice. It was in confirmation hearings for Chief Justice that Roberts used the umpire analogy to support his claims of absolute neutrality, declaring that judges should be like baseball umpires, calling "balls and strikes." He has become so identified with the analogy that he has been called "the umpire in chief." https://www.nytimes.com/2015/06/28/opinion/joun-roberts-the-umpire-in-chief.html.

As the leader of a solid, five vote, very conservative majority, Roberts now finds himself in a position of extraordinary power. The Chief is able to direct the Court and the nation toward the goals he and the other four "conservatives" were nominated to achieve concerning the major issues of the day, including gun rights, affirmative action, voting rights, corporate power, and of course, abortion. Ironically, the sole check on his full-throated use of these powers may be Roberts' concerns as an "institutionalist," reflecting his need, as Chief Justice, to preserve the impartial, non-political, image the Court must have in order to maintain credibility. His vote to uphold portions of Obamacare can be viewed in this light, and it is predictable that any future votes with the Court's "liberal" minority on such sensitive subjects will be, fairly or not, viewed similarly. Put another way, Roberts will have to balance his strong personal and judicial views against the real threat of destroying whatever remains of the Supreme Court's image as a fair and impartial arbiter of the law of the land.

Page 112 — Jennifer Senior, "In Conversation with Antonin Scalia," *New York Magazine*, October, 2013, http://nymag.com/news/features/antonin-scalia-2013-10/index3.html

---

Eric J. Segall, "Does Originalism Matter Anymore?", *The New York Times*, September 10, 2018. https://www.nytimes.com/2018/09/10opinion/kavanaugh-originalism.html

---

Adam Liptak, "An Exit Interview with Richard Posner, Judicial Provocateur," *The New York Times*, September 11, 2017. https://www.nytimes.com/2017/09/11/us/politics/judge-richard-posner-retirement.html?emc=eta1

Page 113 — Linda Greenhouse, "How Judges Know What They Know," *The New York Times*, March 29, 2018; https://www.nytimes.com/2018/03/29/opinion/supreme-court-judges-decisions.html

Page 119 — Judge Irving Ben Cooper's biography can be found at https://en.wikipedia.org/wiki/Irving_Ben_Cooper.

Page 121 — There seems to have been at least one exception to Judge Edelstein's contentious relationship with defense lawyers. As depicted in Matt Tyrnauer's brilliant documentary, *Where is My Roy Cohen?*, in connection with the disbarment proceedings against Cohen that ultimately cost him his law license, Judge Edelstein was

one of numerous, well-connected people to write to the New York
State Bar's Character Committee on his behalf, attesting to Cohen's
honesty, integrity, and good character. www.altimeterfilms.com/
where-is-my-roy-cohen.html.

---

www.nytimes.com/1988/01/18/obituaries/judge-edward-weinfeld-
86-dies-on-us-bench-nearly-4-decades.html

Pages 124–125 — Described in The Almanac of American Politics
as "the nation's best thinker among politicians since Lincoln, and
its best politician among thinkers since Jefferson," it is difficult to
imagine a place for an elected official of his extraordinary intellect
and personal integrity in today's debased, political environment.

A wonderful compendium of Moynihan's remarkable life, including
the quotes appearing in the text, can be found at: https://en.wiki-
pedia.org/wiki/Daniel_Patrick_Moynihan.

Page 126 — <u>Bush v. Gore</u>, 531 U.S. 98, 129 (2000).

Page 127 — Linda Greenhouse, "Playing the Long Game for the
Supreme Court," *The New York Times*, October 25, 2018. https://
www.nytimes.com/2018/10/21/opinion/supreme-court-conser-
vatives-progressives.html

CHAPTER TWELVE

Page 135 — While I do not have the transcript of the Cusack trial, the
quotes come from newspaper accounts, including, *The New York Times*,
May 1, 1999, https://www.nytimes.com/1999/05/01nyregion/man-
is-guilty-of-forging-kennedy-papars-in-a-7-millionscheme.html

The New York Times, May 1, 1999, https://www.nytimes.com/1999/05/01nyregion/man-is-guilty-of-forging-kennedy-papars-in-a-7-million-scheme.html

CHAPTER FOURTEEN

Page 140 — I. Leo Glasser was appointed to the Eastern District of New York bench by President Reagan in 1981 and assumed senior status in 1993. Although a genuine scholar and author of many respected legal writings, he is best known by the public for presiding over the trial of John Gotti. Now in his mid-90s, the judge still hears a select number of cases.

Jonathan Mahler, "All the President's Lawyers," *The New York Times Magazine*, July 5, 2017. Beyond his representation of Donald Trump, Jay Goldberg, a *magna cum laude* graduate of both Brooklyn College and Harvard Law School, has represented celebrities like Bono, Mick Jagger, and Willie Nelson; business tycoons such as Carl Icahn; and mobsters like Matty "the Horse" Ianiello and Pasquale Conte. A complete resume and biography can be found at https://en.wikipedia.org/wiki/Jay_Goldberg.

Page 141 — John Gleeson earned a B.A. degree from Georgetown University in 1975 and his law degree from the University of Virginia in 1980. After clerking on the United States Court of Appeals for the Sixth Circuit, he joined Cravath, Swain & Moore as a litigation associate. He thereafter became an Assistant United States Attorney for the Eastern District of New York. During his prosecutorial tenure, John Gleeson was an active and highly successful trial attorney, principally in organized crime cases. His successful prosecution of mob boss, John Gotti, earned him the Attorney General's Distinguished Service Award. In 1994, President Clinton appointed him to the Eastern District of New York bench.

His tenure on the bench seemed to generate an unusual disparity of opinion among lawyers appearing before him. The strongly divergent views can be seen in posts on a website popular during his tenure, "The Robing Room," created for attorneys to anonymously rate all federal judges. While very few judges receive nearly uniform praise (e.g., Jack B. Weinstein), or almost complete condemnation (e.g., Thomas C. Platt), most judges have reviews that tend to lean substantially one way or the other. The posts on Gleeson, while generally more positive than negative, are especially divergent. The positive include comments such as, "very smart and even-handed judge who lets you try your case;" "a terror as a prosecutor, Judge Gleeson has exceeded expectations as a fair-minded, scholarly and thoughtful judge;" "sharp, smart and quick witted;" and "an excellent judge." The negative evaluations include characterizations like, "self-righteous, "ambitious," "self-promoting," "mean-spirited," and, "high-handed and nasty." http://www.therobingroom.com/Judge.aspex?ID=11. Full disclosure: I posted a strongly negative review of Gleeson on the Robing Room website many years ago, not included above.

Judge Gleeson left the bench in 2017 to become a partner at Debevoise & Plimpton. He is the author of scholarly articles, a lecturer at law schools, and, over the years, a frequent participant in legal seminars and symposia. His strong advocacy for sentencing reform has earned him accolades, particularly from the criminal defense bar.

Pages 143–148 — Official trial transcript, <u>United States v. Pasquale Conte, et al.</u>, 93 CR 0085, E.D.N.Y. (ILG), December 28, 1993, pages 3084-3114.

CHAPTER FIFTEEN

Page 150 — Laurie P. Cohen, Andrew Lucchetti, "NYSE Data at Issue in Trader's Case," *The Wall Street Journal*, May 5, 2008.

Page 152 — "Prison Time Surges for Federal Inmates," The Pew Charitable Trusts, November 18, 2015. https://www.pewtrusts.org/en/research-and-analysis/issue-briefs/201511/prison-time-surges-for-federal-inmates.

Michelle Ye Hee Lee, "Does the United States really have five percent of the world's population and one quarter of the world's prisoners?", *The Washington Post*, April 30, 2015.

Page 154 — Nina Gershon received her B.A. degree in 1962 from Cornell University, and her law degree from Yale Law School in 1965. She was a Fulbright Scholar at the London School of Economics during 1965–66. Judge Gershon was appointed to the Eastern District of New York bench by President Clinton in 1996. Among the many honors and accolades she accumulated over her career, in 1997 she received the New York State Bar Association's coveted Haig Award for Distinguished Public Service.

Mark Hamblett, "Federal Informant Hit with $1.3 Million Verdict," *The New York Law Journal*, Volume 226, No. 74, page one, April 18, 2002.

Pages 154–155 — Robert F. Worth, "Jury Holds an Informer Responsible for his Lies," *The New York Times*, April 20, 2011.

Page 155 — Barry Tarlow, a former federal prosecutor in Los Angeles, first rose to prominence in the late 1960s in numerous high-profile cases, earning the nickname "fighter scholar" and accolades such as the "ultimate advocate." He often appeared as a legal commentator in major media outlets, including, *60 Minutes*, *Nightline*, *Crossfire*, and *Court TV*. A more complete biography, including some of his most well-known cases, can be found at http://wikibin.org/articles/barry-tarlow.html

Pages 155–156 — Elkan Abramowitz has long been considered one of the pillars of the New York criminal defense bar. After graduating from NYU Law School, beginning with a federal clerkship, he had a series of significant government roles, culminating in his 1996 appointment as Chief of the Criminal Division for the United States Attorney's Office for the Southern District of New York, under United States Attorney Robert Fiske. He left government service in 1979 to became a name partner in Morvillo Abramowitz Grand Iason & Anello, one of the leading white collar and civil litigation boutique law firms in New York. Over the years he has represented clients in a host of major white collar criminal matters and significant civil litigations. Among his most famous clients is Woody Allen. *Who's Who of International Business Lawyers* included Elkan among the eight "Most Highly Regarded," calling him a "towering figure." The list of the many honors he has received over the decades includes the Milton S. Gould Award for Outstanding Oral Advocacy by the Office of the Public Defender, *The New York Law Journal's* Lifetime Achievement Award, and the coveted Norman Ostrow Award conferred by The New York Council of Defense Lawyers. The author of too many legal articles and scholarly pieces to list, he is married to the well-known novelist Susan Isaacs.

Page 156–157 — The Second Circuit Court of Appeals, via its official website, now informs attorneys the week before the oral argument of the composition of the panel that will hear their matter. Thus, potential motions to recuse a member of the panel can now be made in a timely manner. It is unclear whether the circuit's website was in operation at the time of the Carriere oral argument, February 2003, and if so, whether it then contained the panel notice feature. The hard copy of the circuit's docket sheet in the case contains no advance notice to counsel of the members of the panel, but that is hardly dispositive. There are, accordingly, three possibilities for our lack of prior knowledge that Gleeson was sitting by designation on the Carriere appeal. Either the website was not yet in operation; there was a website, but the notice function was not yet a part of it; or both Elkan Abramowitz and I (and our firms) somehow failed to search the website the prior week to learn the composition of the panel. The last is an extremely unlikely scenario, especially given the extraordinary importance we attached to who would preside over the appeal.

In any event, Elkan and I are both certain that we first learned of the composition of the appellate panel on the day of oral argument. We each distinctly remember the dilemma posed by the surprise appearance of John Gleeson as a member of the panel, what we discussed, and how we decided to proceed, as recreated in Chapter Fifteen.

Pages 159–160 — The case was overturned on the basis that Judge Gershon erroneously concluded the prosecution against Rothstein was terminated upon a finding that Carriere had lied, not as part of a deal with both Rothstein and Sarnblad. It was an issue not raised at trial and thus not properly preserved by Carriere for appeal. Nonetheless, the panel used it as the basis for its finding. In ruling that Judge Gershon was wrong about the manner of termination of the Rothstein case, Gleeson asserted that the basis for her error was her reliance on the alleged misrepresentations I had made to her, misrepresentations (as established in the record and her letter to the panel) that never took place. See, Rothstein v. Carriere, 373 F.2d 275 (2d Cir. 2004).

Pages 160–161 — Official trial transcript, Rothstein v. Carriere, CV97-7391 (EDNY) (NG), April 9, 2002, pages 283-84.

The basis of the court's overturning the result was "unappealable." Farias v. Instructional Sys., Inc., 259 F.3d 91, 99 (2d. Cir. 2001); See, Rule 50 of the Federal Rules of Civil Procedure.

A final, remarkable disconnect looms over the matter. The only way the appellate panel could have learned of the facts I allegedly concealed from Judge Gershon (i.e., that I represented Donald Sarnblad and that Rothstein paid my pre-trial fee) came from their reading of the trial record, quoted in the text. This was, of course, evidence I presented to Judge Gershon and the jury in open court, and was thus made as clear to her as it was to the appellate panel.

Page 164 — Rather than issuing for publication a new, substitute opinion to remove the baseless allegations, on August 6, 2004, the panel filed an "errata" sheet with the clerk of the court. That minimal filing completely ignored the published opinions' false accusations of misconduct in discovery, but slightly modified its criticism of my trial tactics. My name was mentioned twice, not four times, as though that somehow cured the defects of the original opinion. Thus, even if someone interested in me or the Rothstein case was somehow made aware of, and read the errata filing (unlikely in the extreme), it did little to address the injustice identified by Judge Gershon.

CHAPTER SIXTEEN

Page 168 — Criminal Court of the City of New York, 2016 Annual Report, page 49.

The statistics in states, unlike New York, that fully embraced the "lock 'em up" mentality in their criminal statutes, may well reflect a declining number of trials. To that degree, the "vanishing trial" is an even greater threat.

Page 172 — The total number of cases tried, while obviously significant, is not the only metric for courtroom experience. State cases typically take no more than a week or so to try. This explains how a busy, primarily state court practitioner like Barry Krinsky, can try some 400 cases over his 50-year career. Federal trials, in contrast, especially in major prosecutions, or most any white collar case, usually take much longer. For example, the Ruggiero trial (Chapter Nine) lasted four months before being halted; Conte (Chapter Fourteen) lasted more than one month between opening statements and verdicts; Glass and Joseph (Chapter Nine) took a month to try.

By whatever metric, given that in the pre-Guidelines era nearly 10 percent of criminal cases were tried, and over the decades that followed that number has fallen to some 2 percent, one conclusion is inescapable. The typical lawyer practicing in federal court today, whether prosecutor or defense attorney, has meaningfully less criminal trial experience than his or her predecessors.

CHAPTER SEVENTEEN

Page 175 — Patricia Lee Refo, "The Vanishing Trial," *Litigation*, Volume 30, number 2, page 4, Winter 2004. http://www.abanet.

otg/litigation/home.html

Page 177 — https://www.law360.com/rakoff-slams-us-sentencing-guidelinesfor-being-too-harsh.html.

An honors graduate of Swarthmore College, Jed Rakoff received a master's degree from Oxford and a law degree, with honors, from Harvard. After clerking on the United States Court of Appeals for the Third Circuit, Judge Rakoff entered private practice at Debevoise & Plimpton. In 1973, he became an Assistant United States Attorney in the Southern District of New York, and eventually, Chief of the Business and Securities Fraud Prosecutions Unit. He thereafter returned to private practice, ultimately as a senior litigation partner at Fried, Frank, Harris, Shriver & Jacobson until his 1996 appointment to the Southern District of New York bench by President Bill Clinton. Judge Rakoff has long been a leading advocate of sentencing reform. In perhaps his most famous opinion, in 2002 he declared the federal death penalty unconstitutional, a decision reversed by the Second Circuit Court of Appeals. Since 1988, he has been a lecturer of law at Columbia Law School.

———

The Sentencing Guidelines also eliminated parole, that is, the federal program enabling prisoners to shorten jail time with good behavior pursuant to Parole Board guidelines.

An excellent practitioner's handbook explaining the complexities of the current Guidelines regime can be found in Roger Haines, Jr., Frank Bowman, III, and Jennifer Woll's *Federal Sentencing Guidelines Handbook*, Thompson Reuters, 2018-2019 Edition.

Page 178 — The Pew Charitable Trusts, "Prison Time Surges for Federal Inmates," November, 2015. https://www.pewtrusts.org/

en/research-and-analysis/issue-briefs/2015/11/prison-time-surg-
es-for-federal-inmates

United States Sentencing Commission, "An Overview of Mandatory
Minimum Penalties in the Federal Criminal Justice System," July 2017.

In 2005, after years of disparate legal challenges, the Supreme Court
upheld the constitutionality of the Federal Sentencing Guidelines
by deeming it calculations to be "advisory," not mandatory. United
States v. Booker, 543 U.S. 220 (2005).

Page 184 — Strickland v. Washington, 466 U.S. 668 (1984).

Williams v. Jones, 571 F.3d 1086 (10th Cir. 2009) (*per curium*).

"Sixth Amendment-Ineffective Assistance of Counsel," *The Harvard
Law Review,* Volume 30, No. 7, May 2010, page 1795.

Page 186 — Legislators and academics considering meaningful
changes to the Federal Sentencing Guidelines might find it worth-
while to study the trial statistics in the Northern District of Illinois.
Chicago's Everett Dirksen Courthouse is home to that elite federal
district, which stands as a remarkable exception to the vanishing
trial. As per the United States Sentencing Commission Fiscal Year
2017 Information Packet, the overall national average of federal
court trials was somewhat above 2 percent. The Northern District
of Illinois trial percentage was over 9 percent, by far the highest in
the nation (except the Northern Mariana Islands, an obvious outlier).

Understanding why such an important district produces trial statistics much more in line with the pre-Guidelines era than with the current paucity of trials everywhere else, may help to find a solution to the vanishing trial.

———

The "prison-industrial complex" has long been recognized as a fact of life in the United States. As far back as December 1998, *The Atlantic* reported as follows. "Three decades after the war on crime began, the United States has developed a prison-industrial complex – a set of bureaucratic, political, and economic interests that encourage increased spending on imprisonment, regardless of the need. The prison-industrial complex is not a conspiracy, guiding the nation's criminal-justice policy behind closed doors. It is a confluence of special interests that has given prison construction in the United States a seemingly unstoppable momentum. It is composed of politicians, both liberal and conservative, who have used the fear of crime to gain votes; impoverished rural areas where prisons have become a cornerstone of economic development; private companies that regard the roughly $35 billion spent each year on corrections not as a burden on American taxpayers but as a lucrative market; and government officials whose fiefdoms have expanded along with the inmate population." https://www.theatlantic.com/magazine/archive/1998/12/the-prison-industrial-complex/304669/

In the decades after *The Atlantic* article was published, total annual spending on building, maintaining, and operating prisons in the U.S. has gone up substantially. A 2014 Brookings Institution report put the total figure at $80 billion dollars. http://www.brookings.edu/~/media/research/files/papers/2014/05/01%20crime%20facts/v8_thp_10crimefacts.pdf

Page 187 — *The Washington Post*, "Oklahoma approves largest single-day commutation in U.S. history," https://www.washingtonpost.com/2019/11/03/oklahoma-approves-largest-single-day-commutation-us-history/.

Page 189 — Jeffrey Toobin, "Ben Brafman, The Last of the Big-Time Defense Attorneys," *The New Yorker*, September 1, 2017; https://www.newyorker.com/news/daily-comment/ben-brafman-the-lastof-the-big-time-defense-attorneys.

Page 194 — Francis L. Wellman, *The Art of Cross-Examination*, The Macmillan Co., 1903.

Page 196 — Bob Dylan, "All Along the Watchtower," Columbia Records, released November 22, 1968

ACKNOWLEDGMENTS

My thanks to Elkan Abramowitz, Ben Brafman, Bob Jossen, Ken Kaplan, Barry Krinsky, Scott Leeman, Pat Tuite, and Reid Weingarten. The time you spent, the recollections you shared, and the perspective you provided were invaluable to a meaningful recreation of the past.

Most importantly, to my wife Leslie: your love and support made this book a reality.

Robert Katzberg